France

THE FOURTH REPUBLIC

France

THE FOURTH REPUBLIC

by

Dorothy Maud Pickles

WITH A POSTSCRIPT DESCRIBING
THE SITUATION IN JUNE 1958

GREENWOOD PRESS, PUBLISHERS
WESTPORT, CONNECTICUT

Library of Congress Cataloging in Publication Data
Pickles, Dorothy Maud.
   France, the Fourth Republic.

   Reprint of the 2d ed. published by Methuen, London
issued in series: Home study books, 24.
   Bibliography: p.
   Includes index.
   1. France--Politics and government--1945-1958.
I. Title. II. Series: Home study books ; 24.
[JN2594.P5 1976]   320.4'44   75-3870
ISBN 0-8371-8089-9

This edition originally published in 1958 by Methuen &
Co. Ltd, London

Reprinted with the permission of Methuen & Co., Ltd.

Reprinted in 1976 by Greenwood Press,
a division of Williamhouse-Regency Inc.

Library of Congress Catalog Card Number 75-3870

ISBN 0-8371-8089-9

Printed in the United States of America

PREFACE

FRENCH post-war politics have been much in the news. In the seven years following the referendum in which the French accepted the new constitution, France had fourteen changes of government and as crisis succeeded crisis, it seemed more and more difficult for the Assembly to find successors for defeated governments. There were criticisms of governments, of the constitution, of the political parties, of the selfishness of vested interests, and there was a growing indifference and cynicism among many sections of the population. French criticisms of themselves were reflected in foreign criticisms. There was at times a note of exasperation, of reproach to France for failing during these crucial years to put her own house in order as other war-strained countries had endeavoured to do.

This book does not attempt to supply either a history of or a commentary on post-war politics. It seeks, in the first place, to give a brief and concise picture of the political and economic framework within which the statesmen of post-war France have had to work. That framework was in part inherited from the pre-war years, in part created with the express intention of remedying certain recognized defects of the institutions of the Third Republic. In this book, less attention has been paid to what the French thought about the past, or hoped for from the future, than to the actual working of the institutions as they at present exist, including not merely the formal provisions of the constitution, but also the working of parliament, the relations between the parties, the organization of central and local government and the relations between France and her overseas possessions. It seeks, in the second place, to describe briefly the political and economic problems with which France is at present trying

v

to grapple. It is hoped that the outline will provide an adequate enough background to enable the student of the post-war French scene to interpret more clearly, and perhaps more sympathetically, the often confused and confusing trends of events in post-war France.

I should like to take this opportunity of thanking Professor Kahn-Freund of the London School of Economics and M. Bertrand de la Salle of the French Embassy for their kindness in reading Section (c) of Chapter V and for their criticisms and valuable suggestions.

June 1954.   DOROTHY PICKLES

PREFACE TO THE SECOND EDITION

SINCE this book appeared, there have been many and profound changes in France. At the beginning of 1955, a first constitutional revision had just been completed, but its effects were still unknown. Since then, others have been contemplated; institutions have been modified and some have disappeared; parties have come and gone; the whole concept of the French Union has undergone a sea-change; and the scope and emphasis of French problems, at home, overseas, in Europe and in the world, have changed more than once.

In the present edition, an attempt has been made to take account of the most important of these changes. But in a book of this size some omissions must be inevitable. Moreover, the rate of change in France at the present time is such that few studies of French affairs are fully up-to-date by the time they appear in print. I can, therefore, only apologize in advance for the shortcomings of this one.

March 1958.   DOROTHY PICKLES

CONTENTS

The Government of Post-war France

vii

The Post-war Political Scene

PART I

The Government of Post-war France

★

CHAPTER I

THE HERITAGE OF THE FOURTH REPUBLIC

The instability of institutions. To most British observers, the predominant characteristic of French political institutions is their instability. During the century and a half following the French Revolution, France experienced three further revolutions (1830, 1848 and 1870), two *coups d'état* (1799 and 1851), and three wars (1793, 1870 and 1914), and she was governed by no fewer than eleven distinct written constitutions, three of them monarchic (those of 1791, 1814 and 1830), two dictatorial (those of the year VIII and the year X), three imperial (those of the year XII, of 1815—the *acte additionnel*—and of 1852), and three republican (those of 1795, and of the Second and Third Republics). Some were modifications of existing texts, rather than new constitutions—the constitutions of the years VIII and X, for example—and are, therefore, only formally distinct from modifications of the régime, such as the liberalization of the imperial constitution in 1860 and again in 1870. One of them—the *acte additionnel*—lasted only twenty-one days and so ranks for practical purposes with those constitutions, additional to the ones quoted above, which were never put into application (the two republican constitutions of 1793 and the senatorial constitution of 1814). Nor does the list just given exhaust France's constitutional experiments during this period. For a number of years, she was governed by provisional systems, not based on any written text (the *comité de salut public*, the provisional government of 1848 and the government of national defence of 1870).

Oddly enough, the sixty-five years of the Third Republic, a régime intended by many of those who supported it at its inception to be provisional only, constitute the longest period of time since the Revolution without either a change, or even any profound modification in the constitution. Yet these sixty-five years saw 100 changes of government. During the twenty-three years from the end of the First World War to the French collapse in the Second, the life of French governments averaged only six months. During these years, France had forty-two governments, while Great Britain had eleven.

It has often been pointed out that these frequent changes of government constitute a political ferment that is largely superficial. Governmental changes are often no more than reshuffles which leave a number of ministers in office in several successive governmental coalitions. It was possible, for example, for M. Briand to remain Foreign Minister without interruption (except for one day) from April 1925 to January 1932, during which time there were ten changes of government. Similarly, under the Fourth Republic, M. Bidault remained Foreign Minister from November 1945 to July 1948 (except for one month in December 1946) surviving four changes of government, and M. Schuman was Foreign Minister from July 1948 to January 1953, during which time there were nine changes of government. In fact, from liberation to June 1954, except for the period of interim socialist government of December 1946, France had only two Foreign Ministers and both belonged to the same party, the MRP or progressive catholic party.

No doubt this relative permanence in office of some individual ministers while cabinets change has provided a much greater degree of continuity than is apparent at first sight. No doubt, too, it has tended to increase the prestige within the cabinet of those ministers who survive several changes, and, in particular, the prestige and independence of the Foreign Minister. But in the last resort, it is, of course, the cabinet which is collectively responsible for the determination of policy, and successive cabinets, though they may differ less radically from each other than the British government and opposition, nevertheless do bring some change of emphasis, even where there is no fundamental change of policy. There is no doubt, moreover, that, since the war, the persistence of the habit of governmental instability inherited from the Third Republic has tended to decrease the prestige of France, and therefore of French Foreign Ministers, in international affairs, since their authority has become an increasingly uncertain factor; indeed, their presence at international conferences has, only too often, been prevented by a government crisis.

The stability of public opinion. It has also been pointed out that changes of government are often the reflection of intra-parliamentary rivalries rather than of changes in public opinion. One French writer in particular has argued that the attitude of the French citizen to the basic problems of government, his political way of life, changes so little that it is possible to reduce the different strands making up the pattern of political opinion to two permanent dominating motifs, representing two conflicting national temperaments, whose electoral expression remained almost wholly static throughout the Third Republic. There were, he says, on the one hand the supporters of order, or as we should say, of conservatism and on the other, the supporters of movement—the progressives. In 1877, he says, the supporters of order obtained 45 per cent of the votes; in 1928, 44·5 per cent.[1]

This is perhaps something of an over-simplification. But there are certainly, running through the constitutional experiments and political changes, a number of apparently constant political attitudes. There is, among those sections of opinion whose political inspiration is primarily the Revolution of 1789, a passion for uniformity, a belief in *la République une et indivisible*, and a consequent suspicion of other loyalties, whether regional or professional, but especially of loyalty to the catholic church. There is an unwillingness on the part of parliaments to allow governments to govern, because the basic institution of democracy—the parliament which issues from universal suffrage—is regarded as the supreme organ of government. This belief, not always admitted but nevertheless always there in the background, that executive power must be subordinate to the popularly elected Assembly, not merely in the last resort, but to a great extent in day-to-day matters as well, explains much of the French indifference to the dispersion of executive power in short-lived coalition governments, loosely held together.

Among attitudes more characteristic of conservative opinion, there is the conviction (expressed in the rules governing election to the second house under the constitutions of 1875 and 1946) that age and wisdom are in

[1] François Goguel, *La Politique des Partis sous la IIIe République* (Editions du Seuil, 1946), p. 20.

some way directly related. There is a tendency for the more conservatively minded deputy to feel that he represents less a party, than certain local, professional and individual interests in the constituency, and in consequence is not obliged to submit consistently to party discipline. There is a belief in the essential rightness of individual, often small-scale, private enterprise, and a consequent dislike of state enterprise, a tendency to favour the interests of the producer, and especially of the small producer, as against those of the small consumer, and so to dislike state intervention in the economic field when its aim is to control wages and prices, but to call for it when it seeks to guarantee prices to the producer.

Intellectualism and symbolism. There is, too, in general, a tendency for the French citizen to think of politics in intellectual rather than in practical terms, to attach more importance to symbols than to concrete achievements, to seek to define his position, rather than to promote action to change it, or that of others. 'French politics', said M. Siegfried in 1951, 'are often both unrealistic and passionately ideological.'[1] 'Our legislators', said M. Robert de Jouvenel, 'are far less interested in the contents of the bills before them than in the resolution closing the debate.'[2] A British observer of the behaviour of politicians in the Consultative Assembly of the Council of Europe notes that 'most of them— particularly the Latins—are interested in constitutions rather than functions. They will sketch out the constitutional framework for a transport pool or agricultural pool rapidly enough, but they are bored to distraction if

[1] *Modern France. Problems of the Third and Fourth Republics,* edited by Edward Mead Earle (Princeton, 1951), p. 13.
[2] *La République des Camarades* (Grasset, 1934), p. 89.

they are asked to consider the problems which this machinery should be designed to attack.'[1]

French intellectualism in politics, with its attachment to political symbols, is also strongly historical in its feeling and expression. If the Frenchman cannot fairly be accused of the Bourbon failing of learning nothing, he certainly shares their failing (if it is a failing) of forgetting nothing. 'In French political life', says M. Goguel, 'the past has as great an influence, if not more influence, than the present.'[2] The result is to produce political cleavages which often look to outside observers like echoes of 'old unhappy far-off things and battles long ago'. Anti-clericalism, the individual's resistance to authority (*le citoyen contre les pouvoirs*), the state's reluctance to brook any rivalry in the form of loyalty to other associations—all these are real issues, in the sense that they play a powerful part in current party politics. But the violence of the reactions which such issues set up is due far less to the merits of any particular case than to the accumulated memories of past struggles, to the symbolic importance attaching to them by virtue of their history.

Economic stability. French economic stability, or, as some would say, economic stagnation, has helped to perpetuate these political attitudes. The traditional economy of France is one in which small-scale enterprise is predominant, in both agriculture and industry. France is a country of small towns and villages, of small, scattered farms and small one-man or family businesses.

---

[1] 'Britain and the Consultative Assembly', by Denis Healey, M.P. (*Fabian Journal*, June 1952, p. 17). Mr. Healey was clearly thinking mainly of the French, who were responsible for the drafting of both the projects he refers to.

[2] *France under the Fourth Republic* (Cornell University Press, 1952), p. 140.

Small-town economics have encouraged small-town politics, sometimes directly, as could be seen in the role of the pre-war Senate, whose representation was heavily over-weighted in favour of the village and small town, sometimes indirectly, as, for example, through the pressure of local and professional interests in the parliamentary groups. The inability of French governments to modernize the fiscal system, in spite of repeated announcements of the intention to do so, is due more than to any other single factor to the pressure of those elements in parliament representing the small farmer and the small business man.

The fact that pre-war France grew most of her own food and that a quarter of her overseas trade was with her own empire also contributed to perpetuate these political attitudes. The ordinary Frenchman's way of life was less visibly affected by the activities of governments and parliaments than was the way of life of the average Briton. As Frenchmen themselves often put it, governments might fall, but harvests remained unaffected. France's virtual self-sufficiency in basic foodstuffs also helped to hide from the average citizen the extent to which the French economic system was becoming more and more out of date in the years before the war. It was only after the destruction of the last war, when France's need of outside aid was apparent to all, that the general public began to realize what economists had known for years, namely, that French economic organization was lagging far behind that of the other countries of western Europe. But, as has been said, French habits of thought change slowly. The French citizen's relative lack of interest in economics, his tendency to think of politics in terms of symbols and doctrines, rather than of concrete policies, have survived in a post-war world in

2

which France's situation no longer permits her the luxury of under-production and inefficient distribution.

Changes during the thirties. These are some of the attitudes that go to form the permanent heritage of French politics. The last ten years of the Third Republic and the events of the war years added some new attitudes, and changed the balance of some of the old. Before the war, the most important single change was the gradual discrediting in the mind of the public of the way the parliamentary system worked, and so of the Third Republic itself. The failure of successive governments in the twenties to restore financial stability led to a series of financial crises. Parliamentary government was rendered ineffective, not only by the multiplicity and indiscipline of parties in the Chamber of Deputies, but also by deadlock between the two houses. Under the 1875 constitution, the Senate and the Chamber of Deputies were co-ordinate bodies. Their different methods of election and the longer term of office of the senators (nine years, as against a four-year tenure of office for the deputy) meant that the Senate by no means always reflected opinion in the Chamber. Parliamentary impotence resulted in periods of government by decree (*décrets-lois*). Parliamentary prestige was further undermined by several unsavoury scandals in which the names of deputies were involved and the reputations of some compromised. All this strengthened the opposition to the republican way of life of those elements which had never been enthusiastically democratic and of which some were not even tepidly republican. The thirties saw the growth of a number of authoritarian, para-military, semi- or wholly fascist groups, such as the *Action Française*, Colonel de la Rocque's *Croix de Feu*, Marcel Bucard's *Francistes*, Doriot's Popular Party, and of even more sinister conspiracies, such as that of the Hooded Men.

Proposals to strengthen the hands of governments by increasing the power of the executive encountered the opposition of left-wing opinion, always suspicious of power. Yet the left-wing parties, victorious in the elections of 1936, were themselves unable to carry out their policies fully, owing to the effective veto possessed by the Senate. France's economic backwardness, combined with her unstable finances, made the communist party much stronger than it otherwise would have been, and so seriously divided the forces of the non-communist Left. Both Right and Left were divided on foreign policy, and, in particular, on the policy which ought to be adopted in face of the growing threat from nazi Germany. France entered the Second World War both physically and morally ill-prepared. With the defeat of 1940, the anti-parliamentary forces, temporarily in eclipse as a result of the victory of the Popular Front in the elections of 1936, came into their own again. Vichy France was a right-wing dictatorship, though it was supported by certain left-wing elements which had been either pacifist or in favour of a policy of appeasement. Parliament was suspended, and what power defeated France still had was concentrated in the hands of governments responsible only to the then nearly ninety-year-old Marshal Pétain.

The immediate background of the war years. These years of war and occupation are important as the immediate background to the radical changes introduced by post-war provisional governments as soon as French territory was liberated. Some of them, indeed, were introduced before liberation was complete. The efforts of the Vichy administration to suppress trade unions and to set up corporatist institutions in their place, its contempt for the processes of democratic government and, in particular, for parliamentary government, reinforced the suspicion of the left-wing parties both of personal power in general and of the French right-wing parties. The first elections of liberated France, held in October 1945, resulted in an overwhelming victory for the progressive and revolutionary parties—that is, for the communist, socialist and progressive catholic parties. They proceeded without delay to go much farther along the road on which the first Popular Front government had set out in 1936. State control of the economy, which was for them an article of doctrine, was supported by many other sections of opinion at that time, for reasons of expediency, as the only practicable way of restoring republican and democratic institutions and getting France rapidly back on to her feet again. A series of measures were introduced, nationalizing the mines, the four big deposit banks, electricity and gas. And because the men in charge of affairs after the war blamed the institutions of the Third Republic for the weaknesses that had led to France's defeat, and the men of the Third Republic—or some of them—for collaborating with Vichy or with the enemy, they set out to draw up a new constitution and hoped that post-war France would find new leaders. If the Vichy régime was, as it has sometimes been described, *la revanche de 1936*, then 1944 to 1947 were years which for many elements of the Left constituted *la revanche de 1940*.

The attempt to make a fresh start failed for a variety of reasons. The failure was partly due to the overwhelming difficulties with which a weakened and partially demoralized France was faced after the war. It was partly due to a mistaken analysis of the causes of pre-war failures. The Third Republic was made the scapegoat for deep-seated weaknesses which institutions alone were powerless to eliminate. In fact, the Third Republic had a great deal to its credit. It had come into being at a difficult time, when France had just suffered an ignominious and terrible defeat. It had lasted longer than any previous form of constitutional government in France and had survived four years of invasion and partial occupation in a war which had brought more destruction and involved more casualties than any previous war in history. In spite of all these difficulties, and of internal divisions so deep at times as to render parliamentary government ineffective, it had been responsible for a great extension of social equality and educational opportunity. It had built up a great empire, not always by methods that later generations approved, but which had, at least, included vast expenditure of money and talent in order to improve health and supply education to French colonial subjects.

In so far as the parliamentary institutions of the Third Republic had failed to work well, that failure was attributable less to the form of government than to the nature and extent of French political divisions. As Lord Balfour saw so clearly, parliamentary government can work well only where there is a common desire and will to make it work well. In other words, one of the conditions of its success is a common acceptance of its principles and methods. The Third Republic never succeeded in attracting the full and permanent loyalty of enough of its citizens to ensure that necessary foundation. To that extent, it was always built on sand. Nor did it ever feel secure enough against the threat of German aggression to enable governments to cut expenditure on defence to a level compatible with the country's economic resources. In fact, in this field the policy pursued by successive governments gave France the worst of both worlds. During the pre-war decade she was spending on defence, and, in particular, on the Maginot line, far more than she could afford, but, as later events showed, she was either not spending enough, or not spending wisely enough to protect herself effectively.

The post-war burden. Both these disabilities—internal divisions and external insecurity—were inherited by the Fourth Republic, together with all those problems which the Third Republic had been powerless to solve. It was necessary, for example, to work out the right relationship between legislature and executive, the best way to modernize French agriculture and industry, to reform the antiquated fiscal system and much of the general machinery of administration and to give France a responsible and decentralized system of local government.

In the circumstances, it is hardly surprising that the first decade of the Fourth Republic should not have produced any new or miraculous solution of these long-standing problems. Post-war conditions and the influence of war-time events had combined to make solutions for these and other problems at the same time more urgent and more difficult to achieve. It seemed, for the first year or so after liberation, as if the struggle itself might have helped to eliminate differences between the parties, or at least to narrow them down to a few fundamentals, which could perhaps be allowed to drop into the background while the immediate programme of reconstruction was being carried through. But the unity achieved in resistance did not survive for long, once the single dominant aim of liberation had been replaced by the complex and conflicting demands of peace-time politics. Indeed, it is possible to argue that, on balance, the influence of the war years increased, or at least deepened, existing differences. Bitterness between collaborators (or alleged collaborators) and resisters persisted for years after the war and constituted a new factor of division, cutting across the normal party divisions. It was not until March 1953, over eight years after the end of the war, that the Assembly passed a bill to provide pensions for a number of civil servants, dismissed as a result of the findings of purge committees. It was only in March 1953 that a general amnesty was finally granted to those deputies and senators, who, because they had voted for Pétain in 1940 or had been members of the Vichy *Conseil National*, or had held some official positions under the Vichy government, had been disqualified since the war from standing for parliament. In February 1953, a minister who had held minor office during the period of the Vichy administration was compelled for that reason to resign from M. Mayer's government. In a statement to the Assembly just before his resignation, the unfortunate minister pointed out that he had been acquitted by the *Cour de Justice* of the *département* of the Seine as early as July 1945, and that in rendering its verdict the court had recognized that he had done his duty as a Frenchman and indeed risked 'not only his career, but also his liberty and his life'.[1]

War-time bitterness died hard, and new sources of bitterness arose. The nationalization of the key industries had been agreed on by the underground resistance leaders, but was never acceptable to the majority of conservative opinion. In 1945 and 1946 the conservative parties were too weak to make their opposition felt. As they became stronger, however, they did so with

[1] *Le Monde*, 30.1.53.

increasing emphasis. The failure of post-war governments to arrest the progress of inflation strengthened the opposition of the right-wing parties to the left-wing policy of planned economy and governmental controls, while it strengthened the conviction of the left-wing parties that the best cure for ineffective state controls was more and better ones.

In no field was the legacy of the Third Republic and of the war years more of a burden than in that of economic policy. Out-of-date industrial and agricultural organization, lack of material resources, the absence both of coherent governmental policies and of any clearly discernible majority in the country for any policy—all these combined to render the tasks of successive governments overwhelmingly difficult.

The survival of the Third Republic remained in some doubt for the first twenty years of its existence. The Fourth Republic survived the first decade in infinitely more testing circumstances. But the attempt, in the following pages, to analyse some of France's most pressing post-war problems reveals clearly that victory in the first battles does not yet make it safe to predict with certainty the final victory. For many Frenchmen, the Fourth Republic is still on trial.

CHAPTER II

THE CONSTITUTIONAL FRAMEWORK

The making of the Constitution. In October 1945, the French people decided, by 18,584,746 votes to 699,136, that they would have a new constitution, instead of returning to the constitution of the Third Republic and, perhaps, amending some of its most criticized provisions. A Constituent Assembly was, therefore, elected with an agreed maximum life of seven months. On 19 April 1946 a first draft constitution was passed by 309 votes to 249. It was submitted to a referendum on 5 May and rejected by 10,584,359 votes to 9,454,034. A second Constituent Assembly, elected on 2 June, in the same way and for the same period as the first, passed a second draft on 30 September. The referendum held on the following 13 October resulted in an affirmative vote. Thirty-seven per cent of the electorate voted 'yes'; 31 per cent voted 'no', and 31 per cent did not vote at all. It cannot be said that this represented an enthusiastic reception, but it meant that the constitution of the Fourth Republic was henceforth a fact. It became law on 27 October and entered into force on 24 December 1946.

At first sight, it seems surprising that voters, who, in October 1945, were in favour of a new constitution by 28 to 1, should, in May 1946, have rejected the draft submitted to them by representatives whom they had elected less than seven months earlier and that, after fresh elections had been held, they should still have accepted the amended text so grudgingly. There are two simple explanations. The first is that the Assembly was not elected exclusively as a constitution-making body. It had been decided that the government should remain in power throughout the seven months' period unless defeated by a specific vote of censure supported by an absolute majority of members of the Assembly (that is, half of the total membership, plus one). But the Assembly retained its legislative supremacy. Bills proposing to modify the economic or social structure of the country, the ratification of treaties, and the budget all required its approval before they could become law. In October 1945, electors were, therefore, voting for a particular economic and social policy—for or against the nationalization of certain industries for one thing—as well as voting for a Constituent Assembly.

The second explanation is that the three parties which, between them, polled over 76 per cent of the nineteen million votes cast, though agreed in wanting a new constitution, were not agreed when it came to deciding what kind of constitution it was to be. The result was a compromise that satisfied no party entirely. This had also been the situation when the constitution of 1875 was drafted. Then, however, the majority of the Assembly had hoped soon to replace the republic by a monarchy and had drawn up the provisions with this in mind. Under the Third Republic, the power of the popularly elected Assembly was held in check by a second chamber elected in such a way as to give it a more conservative bias, and enjoying co-ordinate legislative powers. Since there was in fact no return to the monarchy, the changes which the 1875 constitution-makers had hoped to introduce were never made and the Senate remained throughout the sixty-five years of the Third Republic a brake on the power of the Chamber. In 1946, at least 80 per cent of the members of the Constituent Assembly were enthusiastic republicans and over 50 per cent were either socialists or communists. They were determined to see that, in the new constitution, no obstacle should stand in the way of the Assembly elected by universal suffrage. But the agreement broke down when it came to translating this determination into constitutional provisions. Some wanted to go farther than others and to make the elected Assembly virtually omnipotent.

The first draft constitution reflected, in the main, the views of the socialist and communist majority. It provided for a single legislative chamber—the National Assembly. The Prime Minister was to be chosen by an open vote in the Assembly, an absolute majority of its total membership being required.

The President of the Republic, to be chosen in the same way, but by a two-thirds majority, was intended to be a purely ceremonial figure. Conservatives, radicals and the majority of the progressive catholics were opposed to these provisions. 'We believe', wrote the moderate conservative paper, *Le Figaro*, of the first draft, 'that the system will lead to anarchy and incoherence if there is no clear majority and to dictatorship if there is a large majority.' The dominant fear in the minds of ten million electors who voted against the first draft was the fear of dictatorship by the communist party. But they had other objections as well. Following the Revolutionary tradition of 1791, 1793 and 1848, the Constituent Assembly had included in the constitution a Declaration of Rights, reaffirming the political rights proclaimed in the original Declaration of 1789, and adding to them a number of economic and social rights claimed by socialists and agreed to by most of the underground resistance organizations. The right to education (article 25) was formulated in terms to which catholics objected on the ground that they did not specifically guarantee freedom of catholic education. The right to property (articles 35 and 36) was formulated in terms which were interpreted by some conservatives, peasants and small property-owners as constituting a possible threat to the inheritance of private property.

The second draft went some way to meet these objections and so succeeded in winning over sufficient voters (most of them supporters of the progressive catholic party) to ensure its acceptance. It failed, however, to win the support of either radicals or conservatives, for whom it remained too far 'on the side of the revolution', that is, too close to the socialist and communist conceptions which had found their expression in the first draft.

The new constitutional framework. The present system of government cannot be described adequately merely by reference to the content of the 1946 constitution and its subsequent amendments. On some points the parties were unable to reach agreement and the matters in dispute had either to be omitted from the text altogether or phrased non-committally (and sometimes ambiguously), in order to leave the door open for a future settlement. On others, the Fourth Republic was not prepared to commit itself to more than statements of general principle, and left the details to be worked out in subsequent legislation. The institutions of the French Union, the composition of the Economic Council, the High Court of Justice and the Higher Council of the

Judiciary, the electoral system, the constitution of the Council of the Republic—all these are extra-constitutional, in the sense that the constitution either does not mention them at all or mentions them only in general terms and that their constitution and functions are determined by ordinary laws.[1]

On some points neither the constitution nor subsequent legislation provided clarification of the intentions of the Constituent Assembly and the Fourth Republic has simply taken over the traditions and procedure of the previous régime. And there are other points on which the Fourth Republic is creating its own precedents.

There is, in general, a great measure of similarity between the two systems. Like the Third Republic, the Fourth is a parliamentary democracy. It has retained the principle of state neutrality in religious matters, the catholic church and catholic education being maintained from private funds.[2] It maintains the system of direct representation of the overseas territories in the parliament of the mother country. It has also retained the bi-cameral system and an indirect system of election to the second chamber, based on the representation of local government bodies.

The National Assembly consists of 626 deputies,[3] elected for a period of five years, by universal suffrage. Both men and women have the right to vote from the age of twenty-one. Deputies must have attained the

[1] These are described as 'organic laws', but differ from ordinary legislation only in that their content could, with justification, have been included in the constitution.
[2] A law of September 1951 introduced some indirect state aid for catholic schools.
[3] Formerly 627; the Indian Establishments no longer form part of the French Union. The 1956 elections returned only 596 deputies owing to the non-election of 30 deputies for Algeria.

age of twenty-three. The Council of the Republic includes 320 senators, originally called councillors of the Republic, elected for six years, by an electoral college consisting, for the most part, of municipal councillors. Half of the members of the Council retire every three years. Senators must be over the age of thirty-five.[1]

Legislation is considered by both houses. Up to November 1954 all bills were read first in the National Assembly. Now, bills other than money bills and bills to ratify treaties may be read first in the Council (article 14) and during a period of 100 days (or a month in the case of money bills) can pass between the houses to permit the negotiation of an agreed text. If agreement proves impossible, the Assembly's latest text (with or without Council amendments) becomes law (article 20).

The government is made up of ministers, who are usually, though not necessarily, members of one of the two houses and who are chosen by the Prime Minister. They are collectively responsible to the Assembly (but not to the Council of the Republic) for cabinet policy and individually responsible for their personal actions. The President of the Republic is chosen, as were his predecessors during the Third Republic, by the two houses of parliament at a joint meeting, held at Versailles.[2] He holds office for seven years and may not present himself more than once for re-election. He is irresponsible except on a charge of high treason. Like a constitutional monarch, he carries out ceremonial and advisory functions and his political acts require the

[1] Electoral provisions are governed by the laws of 5 October 1946, 3 September 1948, and 9 May 1951.
[2] Under a law of 27 November 1953, voting continues until one candidate receives an absolute majority of the votes cast.

counter-signature of the Prime Minister and of one or more responsible ministers.[1]

1946 compared with 1875. The most immediately obvious difference between the two constitutions of 1946 and 1875 is the diminution both of the legislative authority and of the prestige of the second chamber. Normally, the Council of the Republic has power to delay only for a short time the application of measures decided on in the Assembly.[2] In addition to being a co-ordinate legislative chamber, the former Senate had the constitutional right to give or withhold its consent to a proposal from the President of the Republic to dissolve the Chamber of Deputies. Although this right was exercised only once, in 1877, it has not been entrusted to the Council of the Republic, nor has the Council the right possessed by the former Senate of trying the President on a charge of high treason or ministers on charges of political impropriety.

There are changes, too, in the relations between the government and the Assembly. In the absence of an effective power of dissolution, governments of the thirties were able to govern effectively only by an extensive use of delegated legislation. The system of

[1] Constitutional lawyers report that President Auriol treated the right of pardon as a personal right and that, although he was obliged to ask the advice of the Higher Council of the Judiciary, he did not feel obliged to accept it.

[2] Before the reforms of 1954, the Council could, in theory, block legislation desired by the Assembly, although the authors of the constitution certainly never intended it to possess this power. Article 20 specified that when a bill had been rejected or amended by an absolute majority of the Council, the Assembly, to reassert its own text, must vote it by a similar majority. It was sometimes difficult for the Assembly to obtain sufficient votes to override the Council. If it could not do so, the bill would have to be dropped or to be introduced all over again. *v.* pp. 44–5.

décrets-lois, that is, the right of the government, with the authorization of parliament, to issue decrees having the force of law, enabled governments in effect to dispense with the Chamber of Deputies for a considerable part of the year. The 1946 constitution specifically prohibits the Assembly from delegating its legislative power. It requires governments to resign only when confidence is refused by an absolute majority of the total membership of the Assembly on a vote of confidence or censure, stated in a specific form of words and put after twenty-four hours' notice. And when a parliament has been in existence for eighteen months or more, the government is given the right to dissolve, if it and a previous government have both been defeated within the space of eighteen months, on a vote of confidence or censure put in the circumstances just described. It was hoped that these provisions, together with the elimination of the possibility of deadlock between the two houses, would strengthen the position of governments. But the Fourth Republic, like the Third, discovered that political habits tend to mould institutions, rather than the reverse.

Another change concerned the relations between the Prime Minister and the Assembly. The practice of the Third Republic was for the Prime Minister to be nominated by the President of the Republic and to proceed immediately to form his government, which the Chamber then approved or rejected. The 1946 constitution introduced a new stage, known as the *investiture*. The President's choice was followed by a declaration of policy in the Assembly by the intending Prime Minister (described as *le Président du Conseil désigné*) and that in turn by a debate, in the course of which he replied to questions and objections. Only when the Assembly had approved by an absolute majority of its total membership

the person and policy of the candidate for the premiership (who was then described as *investi*) could he be
officially nominated and form a government. He did not
always succeed in forming one, and, in such cases, the
whole process had to be repeated.

The Prime Minister was, in theory, not required to
submit his choice of colleagues for the approval of the
Assembly. The general tendency, however, was for the
Assembly to endeavour to initiate a debate (that is,
generally speaking, for the communist party to do so)
and for Prime Ministers to resist the attempt. After a
debate which, in practice, turned on the matter in dispute, the vote was usually taken on a motion to adjourn
it *sine die*.

The reforms voted in 1954 abolished the *investiture*
procedure and virtually restored the practice of the Third
Republic. Prime Ministers now ask for the confidence
of the Assembly in themselves and their governments and
the 'constitutional' or absolute majority is not required
(article 45). For a vote of censure, however (or the
refusal of confidence), the requirement of an absolute
majority is retained. The intention of the Assembly was
to make it easier for a new government to be formed,
but not to make it easier for governments to be defeated.
In practice, the reform had little or no effect. During the
three years following it there were four changes of
government. There had been five in the preceding three
years.

The 1946 constitution retained, in the form of a
preamble, the statement of economic and social rights
which had formed articles 22 to 39 of the first draft. This
was a compromise, but, in trying to satisfy both those who
did and those who did not want to include a declaration
of rights, the authors merely succeeded in creating

3

doubts in the minds of constitutional lawyers, politicians and public regarding the precise extent to which anyone was bound by the terms of the preamble. It has been argued that this is not really part of the constitution, that it has moral but not legal validity, that it 'guarantees' the rights proclaimed only in so far as machinery exists to enforce recognition of the principles, and that such machinery is in many cases lacking.

It is true that these rights are formulated only in general terms and that the law does not define precisely either the conditions governing the exercise of many of them or the penalties for their infringement. This imprecision is, however, nothing new in French constitutional history. In previous constitutions which have included declarations of rights, there has usually been a similar distinction between the declaration and subsequent sections of the constitution. For example, the constitution of 1791 incorporated the 1789 Declaration of the Rights of Man and of the Citizen, but, having numbered them articles 1 to 17, it entitled the following section 'French Constitution' and began again at article 1. The constitutions of 24 June 1793 and of 1795 make similar distinctions. Only in the constitution of 1848 is the declaration of rights contained in the body of the constitution (articles 2 to 12). The constitution of 1875 consisted of three short and businesslike laws and included no declaration of rights, but some constitutional lawyers maintained that the principles of the 1789 Declaration were nevertheless constitutionally valid. The preamble of the 1946 constitution, therefore, does no more than perpetuate a confusion that already existed.

New institutions. The constitution of the Fourth Republic provided for the creation of a number of new

institutions—the High Council of the Union, the High
Court of Justice, the Constitutional Committee, the
Higher Council of the Judiciary, and two advisory
Assemblies, the Economic Council and the Assembly of
the Union. The first-mentioned met only three times,
was never important, and virtually ceased to exist after
1953, but something ought perhaps to be said about the
composition and functions of the others.[1]

The constitutions of 1875 and 1946 both recognize the
need for a special court to try the President of the
Republic, if charged with high treason, or ministers, if
charged with offences in connexion with the exercise of
their functions, in cases in which the offence is felt to be
political rather than criminal. The task of trying such
cases was entrusted, under the Third Republic, to the
Senate, constituted for this purpose as *la Haute Cour*.
The reduced power and prestige of the second house in
the Fourth Republic necessitated a change in procedure.

The majority of opinion in the Constituent Assemblies
was in favour of entrusting the responsibility to delegates of the Assembly, henceforth the sovereign power
in the state. The difficulty was that since the Assembly
was to be the accuser, it could hardly with propriety
act also as judge. The solution adopted is the formation,
at the beginning of each parliament, of a High Court of
Justice consisting of twenty deputies chosen by their
colleagues, in such a way that the political complexion

[1] For some description of the composition and functions
of one of the advisory bodies, the Assembly of the Union,
v. Chapter 7. The Higher Council of the Judiciary appoints
and promotes judges and supervises the working of the judicial
system, exercising disciplinary action where necessary. Its
prestige is due in part to the fact that it is presided over by the
President of the Republic, who also nominates two of its
members and to the fact that its advice is necessary before the
President exercises his right of pardon.

of the court is a reflection of that of the Assembly, and of ten members chosen by deputies from outside the ranks of parliament.[1] The court has never been called on to act, although one attempt was made, in 1950, to charge a minister with improperly attempting to hush up irregularities in connexion with the so-called 'affair of the generals'. The proposal failed to obtain the absolute majority required by the constitution (in this case 285 votes, as those deputies who were members of the High Court were ineligible to vote) and the matter was taken no farther.

The creation of a Constitutional Committee was seen by the authors of the constitution as a logical consequence of the primacy of the National Assembly. Since it is possible for the Assembly to override the opinion of the Council, where ordinary legislation is concerned, it would also be possible for it to do so on a proposal which the Council might regard as unconstitutional. The Constitutional Committee was intended to guard against this possibility. Its capacity to do so has not yet been tested.

The constitutions of 1875 and 1946 both lay down a special procedure for constitutional revision. Under the 1875 constitution, however, it was exceedingly simple and no special machinery was needed. If the two chambers were not in agreement, no bill could become law, whether or not it involved a constitutional change. Where they were in agreement, they had only to pass a resolution in each chamber, specifying the proposed

---

[1] The president and two vice-presidents of the court are chosen by secret ballot, as are the six deputies who (with their own president and two assessors, chosen by the Higher Council of the Judiciary) form the preparatory Commission to examine such cases. A two-thirds majority is required for election. These deputies take no part in any decision by the Assembly to bring a minister or ministers before the court.

revision,[1] and then to hold a special session at Versailles at which, sitting together as a National Assembly, they voted the revision already agreed on. In the Fourth Republic, the procedure is still relatively simple, where the two houses are in agreement, though it differs in several ways from that of ordinary legislation. A resolution stating what it is proposed to revise should normally be voted in each house by an absolute majority of its total membership. The proposed changes are then incorporated in an ordinary bill and voted in the normal way by both houses. If the bill receives either a three-fifths majority in each house or a two-thirds majority in the Assembly, the constitutional revision is complete on the promulgation of the law. If the majority is less than this a referendum must be held.

Where the two houses are in disagreement, the constitution requires the resolution to be voted twice by the National Assembly (with an interval of at least three months and each time by an absolute majority of the membership), before the proposed revision is introduced as a bill. If, on its second reading, it obtains a two-thirds majority, the revision is again considered to be complete on the promulgation of the law. If it fails to obtain a two-thirds majority, a referendum must be held.[2]

Where, in the view of the Council of the Republic, the Assembly is treating as ordinary legislation measures which involve changes in the constitution, the President

[1] In each case, an absolute majority of the votes was required. When the two houses met to vote together, an absolute majority of the total membership was required. The first provision ensured that the Chamber should not be able to impose revision against the will of the Senate.

[2] A revision of the constitution relating to 'the existence of the Council of the Republic' requires either the assent of the Council or ratification by the electorate in a referendum.

of the Council of the Republic is empowered, on the authority of a vote by an absolute majority of the membership of the Council, to take steps, together with the President of the Republic, to bring the matter before the Constitutional Committee during the interval which elapses between the passage of a bill in the Assembly and its promulgation as law by the President of the Republic.[1] The Committee endeavours as a first step to get the two houses to agree[2] and, failing this, makes a pronouncement regarding the constitutionality of the measure in question. If declared to be unconstitutional, it is referred back to the Assembly which can either let the matter drop, alter its text in order to make it conform with the requirements of the constitution, or revise the constitution in accordance with the procedure already described.

Like the Assembly of the Union,[3] the Economic Council is an advisory body with a quasi-parliamentary organization. Its sessions, like those of the two houses of parliament, are public and its reports are published in the *Journal Officiel*. Candidates for election must fulfil the same conditions as for election to the National Assembly and, in addition, must have belonged for a period of at least two years to the industry or profession that they represent. The Council consists of 169 members, elected for three years to represent the

[1] The Constitutional Committee consists of the President of the Republic and the Presidents of the two houses, together with seven nominees of the Assembly and three nominees of the Council, chosen from outside the ranks of parliament, who hold office for the duration of the session.

[2] It has been suggested that the Constitutional Committee should be able to intervene in order to point out the unconstitutionality of proposed legislation, even when the two houses are in agreement. The constitution does not seem to make this possible.

[3] *v.* Chapter 7.

principal organized economic interests in the country.[1] Its functions are to advise the government on the working out of a national plan for full employment and to report on the working of such plans when in operation; to advise the government on decrees in application of laws dealing with economic matters on which the Economic Council has been consulted, and on certain general economic questions; and also, when consulted, to advise either government or Assembly on legislation concerned mainly with economic and social matters (with the exception of the budget). The Economic Council is also free to consider economic questions on its own initiative and to transmit its conclusions in the form of proposals to either the Assembly or the government. It has made use of this power very freely and has put forward a large number of recommendations.

Proposals for reform. There was opposition to the new constitution before it came into force and criticisms of its working were fairly general before the end of the first parliament.

General de Gaulle had expressed his opposition as far back as 1946 and the movement led by him put in the

[1] The law of 27 October 1946 setting up an Economic Council provided for 164 members. The law of 20 March 1951 modified both the representation and the functions of the Economic Council. It is now compulsory for the government to consult it on certain general economic questions, whereas originally consultation was optional except in regard to national economic plans. The 169 members are divided into ten categories:

Representatives of labour (45); of industry, commerce and trade (40); of agricultural organizations (35); of co-operative organizations (9); of overseas territories (15); of intellectuals (8); of family associations and housing organizations (9); of associations of sufferers from bomb damage (2); of the middle classes (2); and one representative to represent each of the following interests:—savings, property, exports, the tourist trade.

forefront of its programme the need for constitutional revision, in order to strengthen the power of the executive as against the legislature. On the whole, the right-wing parties accepted the criticisms of the Gaullists, though they did not agree with some of their positive proposals. The radical party had been opposed to the whole idea of a new constitution and remained steadfastly loyal to the political institutions as well as the political habits of the Third Republic.

In November 1950, after prolonged discussion in commission, the National Assembly passed a resolution in favour of the revision of eleven articles of the constitution. The revision was not completed, however, for four years. The delay was due, in part to disagreements about two of the proposed reforms, and in part, to fears that the application of one of them might effect the voting on the E.D.C. Treaty, a subject that dominated the political stage most of that time.

The reform sought to do four things:

(i) to make a number of minor, in the main, technical changes, in order to improve the practical working of the constitution (articles 7, 9, 12, 49 and 50),

(ii) to prevent the communist party from abusing the deputy's right to immunity from prosecution in certain circumstances (article 22) and to reduce the risk of a communist's exercising the functions of President of the Assembly, or being a member of, or perhaps heading, a caretaker government, at what might be critical moments (articles 11 and 52),

(iii) to increase the legislative power, or influence, of the Council of the Republic (articles 14 and 20), and

(iv) to modify the rules governing the *investiture* of the Prime Minister (article 45).

The most contested were those concerned with the *investiture* and the Council of the Republic. It was hoped by supporters of the reform that the first would reduce governmental instability and that the second would make for more fruitful co-operation between the two Assemblies. In fact, the change in the *investiture* procedure had no discernible effect (*v.* p. 23). The Council's position was changed in three ways. First, some bills (excluding money bills) could, henceforth, be read first in the Council; second, the delaying powers of the Council were increased (*v.* pp. 44–5); and third, the conditions in which the Assembly could override the Council were modified. Before the revision of article 20, in order to pass a bill which the Council had rejected by an absolute majority, the Assembly was obliged to vote it on second reading also by an absolute majority. On issues where the Assembly was very divided, this requirement could prove a serious obstacle. Many Senators felt that the suppression of this requirement deprived them of a real, if contingent, power, whilst the increased delaying power (*la navette*) merely gave them the right to prolong an argument without affecting its outcome.

The reforms did not go far enough to satisfy any of the chief critics of the constitution. In 1955, the French Parliament decided to revise a further 28 articles, 23 of them (articles 60–82) concerned with the organization of the French Union. It was not, however, until 1958 that specific proposals were placed before the Assembly and, even then, they dealt with only four articles. The Bill encountered great opposition in the Assembly. Right-wing parties were prepared to agree to constitutional revision only if it were accompanied by electoral reform. Since the latter has been since the war an even thornier subject of dispute than the former, leading, in

1955, to five weeks of abortive debate in the Assembly, followed by a government defeat and a dissolution, considerable doubt was felt ·regarding the likelihood of either reform being speedily accomplished.

The government bill sought:

(i) to withdraw the right of financial initiative from deputies (article 17),
(ii) to prevent governments from being defeated on purely destructive votes of confidence or censure (articles 49 and 50). It was, therefore, proposed that for a government to be defeated in this way, the opposition must put forward an alternative policy and indicate the name of an agreed alternative Prime Minister, and
(iii) to modify the rules governing the dissolution (article 51) in an effort to prevent long governmental interregna, or periods of prolonged deadlock in the Assembly.

Discussion of the proposals, and of the working of parliamentary institutions in general, revealed, from 1955 onwards, a growing dissatisfaction with the situation in France. In 1958, more than at any time since the war, there was increasing disquiet lest the inadequacies of successive governments should lead to a real threat to the régime. In part, this was a consequence of the prolonged failure to solve the Algerian problem and of the economic as well as political dilemmas posed by the continuation of war in Algeria. But it was also, in part, evidence of a genuine growth of interest, not yet among the general public, but certainly in press and Parliament, in the machinery of government and of a genuine desire to improve its working in France.

CHAPTER III

THE PARLIAMENTARY SYSTEM

The electoral system. Elections to the National Assembly.
Among the points of major importance which the
Constituent Assembly left to be dealt with by subsequent
legislation were the systems of election of both deputies
and senators and the constitution of the Council of the
Republic. The election of deputies is governed by
the law of 9 May 1951, which profoundly modified the
system by which the first parliament of the new régime
had been elected in November 1946.[1] Passing new
electoral laws is a traditional pastime of French parliaments, and the unpopular 1951 law was the subject of
much criticism. An abortive attempt by the Assembly to
revise it in 1955 was followed by further discussions
in 1958. The difficulties of reaching agreement were
due, primarily, to conflicting calculations of party
advantages.

Like the two preceding laws governing French post-
war elections, the law of 9 May 1951 provides for a
system of proportional representation, or rather for a
system involving some proportional representation.[2]
For the 627 deputies returned to the National Assembly

[1] Law of 5 October 1946.
[2] During the Third Republic the system of election varied
considerably. In 1919 and 1924 elections were conducted under
a form of "proportional" representation which gave a dispro-
portionately large number of seats to the parties with a majority.
From 1928 to 1940 France returned to the single-member
constituency with two ballots.

in June 1951 were elected in four different ways. The
75 deputies for the 8 constituencies of the *départements*
of Seine and Seine-et-Oise were elected at a single ballot,
by list voting, according to a system of proportional
representation which slightly favours smaller groups.[1]
It was hoped, thus, to mitigate somewhat the domination
of the Paris region by the two rival giants, the communist party and the Gaullist *Rassemblement du Peuple
Français*. The 9 deputies for the three 'old colonies' of
Guadeloupe, Martinique and Réunion were also elected
by this system. The 499 deputies for the remaining 95
constituencies[2] of France and the 8 constituencies of
Algeria were elected by a complicated system intended
to combine the advantages of proportional representation with some of the advantages of the pre-war two-
ballot system. There was, in fact, only one ballot, and
voting was for party lists. Where no party or group of
parties in a constituency obtained an absolute majority,
seats were allocated proportionally (on the 'highest
average' system, which slightly favours large parties).
Any list securing an absolute majority took all the
seats. The new development consisted of electoral
alliances (*apparentements*) concluded on a local basis.[3]
Where an allied group obtained an absolute majority it

[1] The 'highest remainder' system. For a description of its
working see the author's *French Politics*, p. 138.
[2] The constituency is normally the *département*, with from
two to ten seats according to population. The five largest
départements are divided into two constituencies and in one
case (that of the Nord) into three. Finistère returns ten deputies,
Bas Rhin nine, the Loire eight, and so on, down to the smallest
or most sparsely populated *départements* of Basses Alpes,
Hautes Alpes, Belfort and Lozère, which return only two
each.
[3] The local variations occurred despite the fact that the law
made alliances valid only when concluded between parties
having candidates in at least thirty constituencies.

also took all the seats, allocating them proportionally among its member parties. By-elections, on the two-ballot system, were reintroduced. After the 1951 election the communists (who concluded no alliances) and the Gaullists (who concluded only 13) were represented in the Assembly by far fewer deputies than their numerical strength would have entitled them to on either of the proportional systems, if used without the device of *apparentement*. In 1956, however, only 10 *apparentements* enabled allied groups to obtain an absolute majority, partly owing to the appearance of the Poujadists who did not conclude alliances with other parties, partly owing to the bad relations between Socialists and MRP, which meant that in 31 constituencies the democratic parties concluded rival *apparentements*.

The remaining two systems were applied in the overseas territories. Twenty-three deputies for single-member constituencies were elected by simple majority at a single ballot; 21 deputies for 7 West African constituencies and one Equatorial Africa territory were elected on the system of proportional representation in force for both the 1945 and 1946 general elections.[1]

Elections to the Council of the Republic. The rules governing election to the Council of the Republic laid down in the law of 23 September 1948 are even more complicated. There are, in all, five distinct systems of election.

(1) Of the 320 Senators, 246, representing the mother country, are elected by electoral colleges of which there is one for each *département*, consisting of the deputies for the *département*, the *conseillers généraux* and municipal

[1] The 'highest average' system. *v.* the author's *French Politics*, p. 138.

delegates.[1] In *départements* whose population entitles them to four or more senators, election is by list voting and proportional representation (the 'highest average' system);

(2) In the more sparsely populated *départements*, it is by list voting, with a second ballot (at which a simple majority suffices), where no party list obtains an absolute majority at the first ballot;

(3) In overseas territories electing three or more senators the system is that of proportional representation (the 'highest remainder');

(4) In the others the two-ballot system is used.

In most of the overseas territories, French citizens and native electors voted in separate colleges up to 1958.

(5) Nine representatives of French residents abroad (including North Africa and Indo-China) are chosen by the National Assembly, on the recommendation of certain specified bodies. Residents in Morocco are represented by three Senators, in Tunisia by two, in the three Indo-Chinese territories by one.

Senators[2] are elected for six years, a half retiring every three years. Exceptionally, a half of those elected in November 1948 sat for only three and a half years.[3]

---

[1] These are the municipal councillors for towns of from 9,000 to 45,000 inhabitants. In larger towns, the Council elects supplementary delegates; in smaller towns it selects delegates from among the councillors, the number varying according to the population of the town or village. In the overseas territories, the electoral college is normally the local Assembly. Local Assemblies were set up in most overseas territories from 1948 onwards. *v.* Chapter VII.

[2] Councillors of the Republic adopted the former title of senators at the end of 1948.

[3] Elections are held in two series. Series B was renewed in May 1952 (123 senators representing the thirty-seven *départements* from Meurthe-et-Moselle to Yonne, reading alphabetically, and 37 representing specified overseas

Criticisms of the system. Seen through British eyes, these electoral rules seem almost unbelievably complex. It must be admitted, however, that the French elector seems to be able, not merely to grasp the complications, but even to work out the most elaborate calculations regarding the possible electoral consequences of this or that course of action. Indeed, one party in 1951 frequently advised its supporters to vote in the most 'useful' way (*voter utile*), which usually involved a good deal of complicated ' mathematics.[1] If the French elector does not want to go in for abstruse calculations of this kind, the party will do the mathematics for him and all he has to do is to vote the straight party ticket.

The complexity of these electoral systems may be, in part, a consequence of the profound and numerous political divisions in the country, but it also helps to perpetuate the divisions, since proportional representation tends to exaggerate divergencies instead of encouraging compromise. Political habits, however, cannot be changed easily and it is not easy to see a way of breaking this ideological-electoral vicious circle.

The system of election to the Council of the Republic is open in addition to the criticisms often made of its predecessor, the Senate of the Third Republic. It overweights the representation of small rural areas. The overwhelming majority of electors are municipal councillors, or their delegates, and the local electoral system gives the small village many more councillors than the large town, in proportion to their respective

territories); Series A including 123 senators representing *départements* from Ain to Mayenne and 37 representing the remaining overseas territories was renewed in May 1955.

[1] For details of how the system worked, *v.* the author's *French Politics*, Chapter IX and Appendix I.

populations.[1] Then, every *département* has at least one senator and only the six largest *départements* have more than four. The Cantal, with 187,000 inhabitants, and the Allier with 373,000 are each represented by two senators. The system of indirect election also tends to make the Council less representative than the Assembly. There may be a time-lag of as much as ten years between the date of election of municipal councillors and the replacement of the senators whom they elect. Thus, senators elected in 1952 were elected by municipal councillors themselves elected in October 1947. There were important shifts of opinion between 1947 and 1952. The RPF, for example, was still a new movement in 1947 and did not present candidates in most of the rural *communes*. In 1952, it was the second largest party in the country. Yet the senators selected in 1952, and already somewhat unrepresentative of opinion in the country, did not come up for re-election until 1958.

The reduced status of the second chamber in the Fourth Republic lessens the seriousness of these objections, but they cannot be entirely dismissed, partly because the Council of the Republic has steadily grown in prestige, and partly because it possesses a delaying power which, in certain circumstances, can hold up the passage of a bill for some months.

---

[1] *v.* Chapter VI. Of the 102,000 or so electors in metropolitan France, 544 are deputies, 3,028 departmenal councillors and over 90,000 municipal delegates, of whom over three-quarters represent small villages with populations of under 1,000. In the *département* of Meurthe-et-Moselle, for example, of 1,455 electors, 6 are deputies, 29 departmental councillors and 1,420 municipal delegates representing 599 *communes*. Two-thirds of the population live in 592 small villages and have 1,200 to 1,300 delegates, whereas the remaining third is represented by under 200. The Council of the Republic is really elected, therefore, by the representatives of village Councils.

The elected Assemblies. The French parliament presents a very different picture from that presented by the British House of Commons. Of the 627 members of the 1951 National Assembly, a third represented the non-democratic extremes of Gaullism and communism, while the 400 or so members of the parties in favour of the present régime were split into seven parliamentary groups, representing four main tendencies. In the 1956 Assembly 25 per cent of the deputies (then reduced to 596, owing to the postponement of elections in Algeria, and the transfer of the Indian Establishments to Indian sovereignty) were communists and fellow-travellers, 8 per cent (later reduced to 5 per cent) were Poujadists and only 5 per cent represented the former Gaullist movement (now disbanded, the parliamentary rump describing themselves as Social Republicans). The remaining 370 or so deputies included nine political tendencies, divided into a predominantly left-centre and a predominantly right-centre *bloc*.

The occupational break-down also presents a very different picture from that presented by the House of Commons, where in 1951, 156 M.P.s were listed as business men (two-thirds of them company directors or managers), 12 as barristers or solicitors and 59 as representatives of journalism and the medical profession. In the 1951 National Assembly, 51 deputies were described as representing industry and commerce (of whom 30 were listed as *industriels, chefs d'entreprise*), and there were 55 representatives of managerial and office staffs. Eighty-one deputies represented the legal profession, of whom 67 were barristers; 38 represented the medical profession and 39 were journalists or men of letters; past or present civil servants numbered 38 and there were 72 members of the teaching profession.

4

In other words, the liberal professions—legal, medical, pharmaceutical and journalistic—accounted altogether for over a quarter of the membership (158) while state employees—teachers, soldiers, civil servants, railway and Post Office workers—accounted for almost another quarter (131). The British House of Commons included only 18 former civil servants and 47 teachers. Skilled and unskilled workers, who numbered 109 in the British House of Commons, numbered only 47 in the French Assembly, but the latter included 66 representatives of farming and wine-growing, as against only 17 farmers in the House of Commons.

The post-war French Assembly is thus a body consisting predominantly of small functionaries, teachers or civil servants, members of the liberal professions and farmers. Its members have also strong links with local government in their constituencies. Between 200 and 300 members of the two Assemblies—that is, upwards of a third—are also members of their *Conseil général*, while a third of the senators and a quarter of the deputies are also mayors.[1] These professional and local attachments exercise a strong influence on the conduct of parliamentary affairs. The double pull on the loyalty of these deputies contributes in no small degree to the indiscipline which often characterizes the behaviour of individual deputies as members of parliamentary groups.

The organization of parliamentary business and the rules of procedure are laid down for the most part in the standing orders which each house draws up for itself. They are more precise and detailed than the rules governing the procedure of the House of Commons,

[1] *v.* Chapter VI for a description of the active role played by the French mayor in the administration of the *commune*.

because the French prefer to have rights and duties stated clearly in black and white, whereas the British often prefer to rely on unwritten traditions. The French are not prepared to entrust either to the government or to the Presidents of their Assemblies the amount of discretion which the British allow to the government and the Speaker respectively.

Parliamentary sessions now begin on the first Tuesday in October and may be closed by the government after seven months, plus the total period of any interruptions of more than eight full days each. The Council of the Republic, the Assembly of the Union and the Economic Council may sit only when the Assembly is meeting. In practice, the two advisory bodies meet less frequently than the two houses of parliament. Parliament used to sit from January to March or April, from the middle of May to the end of July and from the middle of October to the end of the year or beyond.

The first task of each house at the beginning of the session is to elect the *Bureau*, which comprises the President, the Vice-Presidents, the Secretaries and the *Questeurs*.[1] Until the President has been elected, the National Assembly is presided over by the oldest deputy (the *doyen d'âge*), whose function is to make an opening speech. The President is elected by secret

[1] The Secretaries are responsible for the accuracy of the official record (in practice this is done by officials) and the *Questeurs* for the smooth functioning of material arrangements. The *Questeurs* are usually chosen from among the youngest deputies. There are six Vice-Presidents, fourteen Secretaries and three *Questeurs* in the Assembly, and four Vice-Presidents, eight Secretaries and three *Questeurs* in the Council. In case of a dissolution before the expiry of the Assembly's term of office, the first Vice-President would replace the President during the interim period preceding the formation of a new government following the elections. (Art. 52.)

ballot,[1] and the remaining officers are chosen from a list agreed on by the Presidents of the political groups.

Each house is organized in political groups. The constitution of the parliamentary Commissions—indeed, the whole organization of procedure—is based as far as possible on the principle of proportional representation of political opinion. Groups with less than 28 members (14 up to October 1958) do not constitute organized groups and are not represented in Commissions, unless they ally themselves to some other group for this purpose.

Legislative procedure. Legislative procedure differs in several important ways from that of the British House of Commons. Bills may be introduced either by the government (*projets de loi*) or by private members (*propositions de loi*) of either house and, up to the end of 1954, had to be debated in the National Assembly before being considered by the Council. It is now possible for the Council to vote many bills first. Much legislation, often both important and controversial, is introduced by private members.

After the formal introduction of a bill, its text is printed and distributed and is then studied by the appropriate parliamentary Commission, before being debated. There are nineteen permanent parliamentary Commissions in the National Assembly, dealing with finance, foreign affairs, labour, defence, and so on. Each includes forty-four members and their composition—which must reflect the strength of groups in the Assembly—is determined each year at the opening of the session, in effect by the political parties.[2]

The Presidents of the different Commissions are

[1] A relative majority is sufficient at the third ballot, if two ballots have failed to give any candidate an absolute majority.

[2] There is also the Commission on parliamentary immunity (set up in 1949) consisting of twenty-two members.

shadow ministers (though they do not form a shadow cabinet), in the sense that the President of the Commission and not the relevant minister is responsible for piloting a bill through the house, and the Assembly debate opens, not with a ministerial declaration, but with the Commission's report.

The Commissions have great prestige. They frequently interrogate ministers from whom they obtain clarification or information; they have access to documents, and so are in a position to challenge the government's case on the basis of the minister's own data. When a British bill enters the committee stage, its general outline has already been decided, for good or ill, by M.P.s, many of whom know little or nothing about it and have simply voted as their party directed. But when a bill comes before the French Assembly for debate, there is, as a result of the Commission's work, an informed body of opinion in the house able to discuss it both in principle and in detail.

The French system has its own disadvantages, however. The fact that the Commission reflects the political complexion of the house and that its President may be a member of the party to which the minister belongs does not protect the government from criticism which may even go as far as presenting the Assembly with a report which constitutes, in effect, a counter-proposition. In other words, it not infrequently happens that the ordinary member hears the case against the government's version of the bill before he hears the case for it. A minister whose first encounter with the Assembly consists of a trial of strength between himself and the Commission, in which the Assembly is called on to decide whether the government's or the Assembly's text is to form the basis of the debate, is on the wrong foot, so to speak, from the beginning. He is defensive rather than expository and he is often fighting for his life—or that of the government—instead of for his bill, although the bill has already been accepted by a cabinet which has, theoretically, a majority in the Assembly.

It is true that the views of a minister, as a member of a coalition cabinet, are often a far from accurate reflection of his views as a party member. He is, therefore, not always averse to pressure from his own party in the house. But such pressure can and does seriously weaken the cabinet's authority and often destroys collective responsibility. In the French mind, however, parliament is a ground on which two battles are taking place simultaneously, sometimes to the confusion of all protagonists. There is the battle between those parties, most of whose members support the government of the moment, and those who, in the main, oppose it. But there is also the battle between the legislature and the executive, between the representatives of the citizen and those of the state.

After the general debate on the Commission's report, the Assembly debates and votes on the bill, article by article, and finally votes on the complete text, as amended. This is the Assembly's first reading. The bill then goes to the Council of the Republic where it goes through the same stages. If the Council of the Republic passes it, it is promulgated by the President of the Republic and published in the *Journal Officiel* and is then law. If the Council amends or rejects the bill, however, the Assembly gives it a second reading. If there is still disagreement, the bill passes from one Assembly to the other (hence the name, *la navette*), for a period varying according to circumstances from 15 to 100 parliamentary days from the time it is received by the Council for a second reading. If, at the end of that period, agreement has still not been reached, the Assembly has the last word, being free either to vote the text as it stood at the Assembly's last reading, or to incorporate in it any Council amendments that it chooses. Before the 1954 revision, the Council had merely the right to amend or reject the Assembly's text 'in whole or in part', and the Assembly was entitled, on its second reading, to reconsider only those parts which had been amended or rejected by the Council, which had to be either accepted or rejected, but could not be further amended.[1] If the Council had rejected the bill outright, the Assembly could either vote its own text a second time, or let the bill drop, or introduce a new bill and go through all the stages again. The revised procedure gives the Council, if not more power, at least the possibility of more influence, and has the advantage of giving both Assemblies opportunities for second and third thoughts. But in cases of acute disagreement between the two Assemblies, it also, of course, enables the Council to delay the passage of a bill for a period that, if allowance is made for parliamentary vacations, may be nearer 200 than 100 days.

The characteristics of debate. Debates in the Assembly tend to be at the same time more formal and less orderly than those of the House of Commons. In what is called an 'organized' debate, the time allotted to spokesmen of the different parties is worked out in detail and not, as in Great Britain, left to negotiations between the Whips and to the discretion of the Speaker. Members do not

[1] There were a number of attempts to get round the obstacles created by this rigid relationship between the two houses, some of them unofficial, some involving debateable interpretations of the constitutional rules regarding the procedure to be followed, some involving highly complex linguistic acrobatics.

speak from their seats across a narrow gangway but from a raised platform (*la tribune*) just below the President's chair. They thus face assembled members seated in a semicircular amphitheatre, from right-wing deputies on the right to communist deputies on the extreme left. The government occupies the two front rows of the centre stalls, so to speak, Presidents and *Rapporteurs* of Commissions the two front rows on their right. Speeches are more formal and oratorical than in the British House of Commons. They are punctuated by applause (or abuse) and members sometimes rise to their feet at the conclusion and give the speaker a prolonged round of applause. When the vocal expression of opinion takes a critical form it can very soon get out of hand and, from the banging of desk-lids (which can drown the sound of the President's hammer, designed to call deputies to order), become rapidly a free fight in which combatants have to be forcibly separated by the detachment of the Republican Guard always on duty in the precincts of parliament. Debates in which party feeling rises high are sometimes suspended several times in order to allow tempers to cool. An American magazine estimated that, in 1951, the communists and their opponents came to blows on thirty-seven occasions.

The French Assembly attaches much more importance than does the British House of Commons to the expression of opinion by all sections of opinion and in proportion to their numerical representation in the Assembly. In an 'organized' debate, time is rigidly allotted on this principle, though the schedule is rarely observed in practice. Before a vote is taken every group has usually the right to address the Assembly for five minutes in order to explain the reasons why its vote is to be cast this way or that (*l'explication de vote*). In an Assembly with a dozen or more organized groups, this process if frequently repeated can take up a considerable time and all-night sessions are, therefore, frequent. In March 1950, during a debate on the bill to repress sabotage, the Assembly sat uninterruptedly for over three days, except for short suspensions, necessary to restore order.

Voting procedure. Voting in the Assembly can be either by show of hands, by standing up, by ballot (with or without a subsequent check—*pointage*) or by open ballot at the *tribune*. A vote by ballot is held normally when the decision is of some importance and deputies, therefore, desire a record of the way they have voted. Deputies vote, not by going through lobbies, but by placing a card with their name on it in an urn. A white card denotes a vote *for*, a blue card a vote *against*. Deputies may also inform the President of their intention to abstain from voting, which is not the same thing as not voting, but a positive declaration of neutrality. There is no system of pairing, but proxy voting is allowed, except for important issues, such as investiture and votes of confidence or censure, when the deputy has been obliged, since a change in the Standing Orders of July 1955, to vote personally. Normally, the secretary of the group is entitled to cast the votes of the whole group (the method invariably used by the communists). It does, of course, sometimes happen that more than one proxy votes for a deputy. The secretaries therefore sort out the bulletins and see that only one vote per deputy is recorded before the result is announced. If a proxy votes in a way contrary to the intention of the deputy, or if the deputy himself changes his mind, two courses of action are open to him. He can either put two bulletins of the opposite colour in the urn, thus cancelling his original vote and substituting another, or he can notify the *bureau* of his real intentions after the vote has been taken. The printed 'rectified vote' will then record his final decision. The 'rectified vote' does not, however, affect the issue. It may, therefore, happen that a vote giving the government a majority turns out, after rectification, to have been a government defeat. The value of the rectification is twofold. First, it allows a deputy to correct what may have been a real mistake regarding his intentions and so safeguards his position *vis-à-vis* his constituents. Second, it allows a deputy who does not know quite what to do to have the best of both worlds. He votes one way and then proclaims that he really intended to vote the other way!

Where a further check is called for, a more leisurely and closely supervised count is made. In matters of great importance—or where one party is anxious to waste time—an open ballot at the *tribune* may be demanded. In this case the deputy must mount the *tribune* and deposit his vote in person. As there are 627 deputies and a majority must be present for such a ballot to be held, it will be evident that the process takes up a considerable amount of time—from one to two hours. For this reason, use of the open ballot has been restricted, since March 1952, to a few specially enumerated cases.

Questions. As in Great Britain, members of parliament may put both oral and written questions to ministers and written answers are published in the *Journal Officiel*, but questions are less frequent and there is nothing equivalent to the political battle of wits characteristic of question-time in the House of Commons. The Assembly also has the right to question the government on its general policy (the process known as *interpellation*). The Council of the Republic does not possess this right, but the procedure known as 'oral questions with debate' is an *interpellation* in all but name, with the significant difference, of course, that the government is not affected by an adverse vote since it is not responsible to the second chamber.

The relations between the Government and the Assembly. The British system of parliamentary government is sometimes criticized on the ground that the backbencher is tending to become a rubber stamp, only slightly less at the mercy of party discipline when his party is in opposition than when it is in office. The French system is often criticized on the ground that governments are at the mercy of an indisciplined and often capricious Assembly, to an extent that renders their tenure of office precarious and their exercise of power uncomfortable. It is relatively simple for deputies to avoid placing themselves in a position in which the special provisions of the constitution for a dissolution can be applied, and governments have not been anxious to apply them either. The deputy who is elected for five years can normally count on remaining in parliament for the full five years, however many governments come and go during that time. Pressure on a government from the fringe of its own supporters is, therefore, something that has to be taken into account, for the government can be threatened by a handful of potential rebels.[1]

Indeed, French parliamentary procedure favours the Assembly at almost every point. The time-table is not, as in Great Britain, controlled by the government (with the safety-valve of agreement between the Whips) but is drawn up at a meeting (usually weekly) of group leaders and Presidents of Commissions (*la Conférence des Présidents*), and agreed to by the Assembly; private

[1] But *v*. p. 53 on the 1955 dissolution.

members dispose of much more time to introduce legislation and, on the average, a quarter of the bills voted in a session have been introduced by private members. Deputies have the right to propose expenditure, though not during debates on the Finance Bill. In practice, they often do so even then, because the Finance Commission does have the right and has been known to unbalance the government's budget (assuming it to have been balanced in the first place, which has not always been the case since the war) by presenting to the Assembly proposals for increased expenditure, accompanied by highly theoretical and unrealistic provisions for raising the necessary revenue. Commissions, as has been said, often put to the Assembly alternatives to the minister's bill, which amount to counter-propositions. Debates can be curtailed only with the agreement of the Assembly and 'organized' only if the Assembly so decides. The President has neither the Speaker's power to select amendments, nor his discretion in calling on speakers, nor his authority in calling to order a deputy who is being irrelevant. Deliberate time-wasting is, therefore, possible. In 1950, for example, a communist deputy spoke for over five hours in the debate on the anti-Sabotage Bill.

The post-war Parliamentary crisis. This supremacy of the legislature has been criticized, in the main by right-wing parties, as being directly responsible for governmental instability and weakness. Suggestions to strengthen the power of the executive have hitherto been resisted, however, by the parties on the Left, who as legatees of the Revolution, are more afraid of executive power than of *gouvernement d'assemblée*. Governmental instability has been, for several reasons, a more serious handicap to the Fourth Republic than it was to the Third.

Divisions between parties have been more complex, the world situation has been more difficult and France's problems, both at home and overseas, have been more intractable than during the pre-war years.

The result has been that the government's main—indeed almost its only—weapon against the Assembly has usually been purely and simply the threat to resign. In the relative stability of pre-war economic and political life, a government's resignation was not an event of major importance, since there was always an available alternative combination within the framework of parliamentary government. In post-war France, the extreme parties have comprised from a quarter to a third of the Assembly. The margin within which democratic and parliamentary government can operate has, thus, greatly narrowed and, when socialists have been in opposition—or in a limbo of more or less benevolent neutrality—there has been in the main only *one* workable governmental combination, namely, a coalition of all the remaining non-extremist political parties. Governments in post-war France have tended, therefore, to be combinations of the possible rather than the desirable and government defeats or resignations have been followed, more often than not, by 'the mixture as before'.

The coalition parties have been, nevertheless, deeply divided on economic and social policy and sometimes on foreign policy and their acute electoral rivalry has often exacerbated these differences. The result has been to create a state of affairs which, to Anglo-Saxon eyes, has something schizophrenic about it. The more the French elector attaches importance to voting for exactly what he would like, as expressed in the mathematically precise differentiation of a whole gamut of electoral opinions, the less say he has in reality, in what he gets, in terms of governmental policy. For the compromises which are an essential condition of parliamentary government have to be made after the election.

In Great Britain, where members of parliament are elected to support one of two national programmes, there is only one political battle in parliament and in the country—that between government and opposition. In France, there are four, even five, if we include the permanent divisions on doctrinal questions that differentiate Left and Right. There is, in addition to the battle between government and opposition, and between deputies and government—that is, between legislature and executive—the struggle between the parties making up the coalition both in the government and in the Assembly. Each party has to try to get as much of its programme accepted as possible, but compromises reached in the cabinet are not always accepted by the rank and file, which can bring pressure to bear in Commission, in debate, and finally by refusing to vote for the government.

The fifth battle is that which takes place within the mind and conscience of the individual deputy, torn between his loyalty to his constituents and his loyalty to his party. The back-bencher has always played a more important role in France than in Great Britain, because individualism is stronger and parties, in general, are more loosely organized. The fragile majorities of post-war governments have increased the deputy's importance, since one or two dissident votes can bring down a government. At the same time, the system of proportional representation, with constituencies of several hundred thousands of electors, has increased the deputy's dependence on the party machine. The position in post-war France is that the deputy needs the party in order to be elected in the first place. But once he is a member of the Assembly, the party often needs him more than he needs it. It needs him, for example, in order to maintain its cohesion and so exercise its maximum bargaining power.

The Right and some of the Centre believe that the governmental authority over the Assembly can be increased by the use of the instrument of dissolution. The Left has always disliked dissolution and its use in 1955 only strengthened their feeling. In fact, the circumstances helped to discredit it (as they did in 1877, the only other instance of its use) and the consequences, if they prove anything, demonstrated its irrelevance to the solution of French problems. For deadlock in the Assembly and divisions in the government were even more marked in the 1956 Assembly.

For many Frenchmen, the crying necessity is rather that parties should abandon their doctrinaire attitudes and paralysing intransigence and so enable the country to find a way out of the post-war governmental impasse, through new electoral groupings based on specific programmes. For others, this statement of the problem confuses cause and effect. They hold that parties are intransigent precisely because, and to the extent to which, their interests and aims are incompatible and irreconcilable. If this is so, then the conditions of stable parliamentary government may not be present. Others again hold that the governmental impasse is due less to the fundamental divisions between parties than to the acute rivalry which inevitably results from their more or less equal electoral strength. Some account of the strength, organization and outlook of the post-war parties is therefore vital to the understanding of the working of post-war political institutions.

CHAPTER IV

THE POLITICAL PARTIES AND
THE TRADE UNION MOVEMENTS

The general picture. To anyone unfamiliar with French party politics, nothing could be more confusing than to consult election results and the official lists of parliamentary groups in the Assembly and the Council of the Republic. Some parliamentary groups have little or no

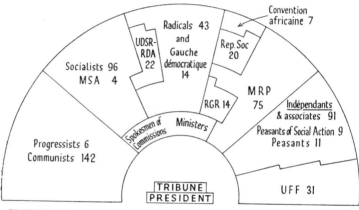

SEATING OF GROUPS IN THE NATIONAL ASSEMBLY, APRIL 1958

Note. *The 30 Deputies for Algeria were not elected in January 1956. The Assembly therefore numbers only 596 Deputies, of whom 11 belong to no group and are not shown because they do not sit together.*

extra-parliamentary organization, while some party organizations have no parliamentary equivalent. Parties and deputies sometimes fight elections under labels different from those that they adopt in parliament. Some electoral labels represent ephemeral coalitions

54

that do not survive the election. In the 1951 election, two alliances called respectively, *Union des Indépendants Paysans et Républicains Nationaux*, and *Rassemblement des Groupements Républicains et Indépendants Français*, each presented candidates in more than thirty *départements*, but disappeared under those names immediately after the election. M. Cot, a member of a fellow travelling parliamentary group (the *Républicains Progressistes*), which has little extra-parliamentary existence, was elected on the communist party list, which, incidentally, was entitled 'Republican, Resistant, anti-Fascist Union for National Independence, Bread, Liberty and Peace'. In the 1946 parliament, twenty-seven deputies belonged to a right-wing group called the PRL (*Parti Républicain de la Liberté*). In 1951, this group was not mentioned in the election results, nor was there a group with this name in the 1951 Assembly.[1] But in the 1956 Assembly some 30 deputies constituted a new and much more extreme right-wing group, *Union et Fraternité Française*, more popularly known as Poujadists.

The confusion, though real, is nevertheless reduced relatively easily by the French elector to some sort of order. Some 70 per cent of French electors vote for one of six major political tendencies. Three of them (conservative, radical, and socialist) have been permanent features of Republican France since the beginning of this century, the fourth (communist) since the end of the First World War. The fifth, the progressive Catholic tendency, is represented by the MRP (*Mouvement Républicain Populaire*), formed during the occupation as a clandestine resistance movement, though its spiritual origins are two small Catholic parties of the pre-war years. The sixth is made up of a number of different

[1] For changes in parties, see Appendix 3.

5

elements, having in common only their opposition to the régime, and sometimes to parliamentary government itself. The RPF (*Rassemblement du Peuple Français*) was founded by General de Gaulle in 1947, contested the elections of 1951, when its candidates received over four million votes (21 per cent)[1] and its representatives constituted the largest party in the Assembly. In 1953, General de Gaulle withdrew support from the parliamentary movement and, in 1955, the RPF organization in the country was disbanded. The parliamentary group, now known as Social Republicans, was reduced after the 1956 elections to 21. The 1956 Assembly included, however, for the first time since the war an extreme right-wing element, represented by the Poujadists and by three deputies calling themselves 'The New Right', one of a number of small, extremist, mainly extra-parliamentary and anti-parliamentary movements formed between 1951 and 1957. Most of them claimed only a few hundred supporters. Their existence was, however, symptomatic of the growth of dissatisfaction with the régime.

The Communists. With nearly five and a half million electors out of a total electorate of over 26 million,[2] the communist party is by far the strongest party (and also the largest in the 1956 Assembly) and its electoral strength has varied very little since the war. It lost some 400,000 votes in 1951, and gained half a million in 1956, but with an electorate increased by over two million. Communist strongholds in the Paris region (the red belt), the industrial north-east, parts of the *massif central* and

---

[1] For changes in parties, see Appendix 3.
[2] Electoral statistics refer only to France. Figures relating to seats in the Assembly or in the Council of the Republic include overseas representatives unless otherwise stated.

the coastal *départements* of the south-east, remained virtually unaffected. The communist party was the only one to have a minimum of 5 per cent of electors in every *département* and it had over 30 per cent in more *départements* (31) than did any other party. In spite of an electoral system heavily biased against them, communist deputies numbered almost a quarter of the Assembly.

Party membership is, of course, much smaller. At its peak, in 1947, it was estimated at 800,000 and for a few months even reached a million. Since then it has fallen, and in 1958 was estimated to be well under half a million. The circulation of the Paris daily paper *L'Humanité*, estimated shortly after the liberation to be over 400,000, had fallen, in 1953, to about 154,000 and the communist evening paper *Ce Soir*, which, in 1949, had a circulation of 250,000, ceased publication early in 1953. The party has, however, a score or more provincial papers with large circulations. The leading trade union confederation, the CGT (*Confédération Générale du Travail*), has been communist-dominated since 1947.[1]

As a Marxist, workers' party, the communists are in favour of state control of the means of production and of the handing over of land to the peasants. In a country like France, with a large population of highly individualistic peasant landowners, any talk of land nationalization or collective farms would be electoral suicide. The party's post-war headway in some rural areas with a relatively high proportion of farmers has been achieved partly by exploiting local grievances, partly by slogans promising 'the land to those who work on it'.

[1] See pp. 85–8. Both party and trade union organizations lost members after the suppression of the Hungarian revolution.

In day-to-day politics, the communists have consistently supported claims for increases in wages, except for a short period in 1946 when they were represented in the government. Apart from that, it is easier to describe what the party is *against* than what it is *for*. It is anti-American, was opposed to Marshall and military aid, to the war in Indo-China, to German rearmament and European integration. It has followed Moscow directives undeviatingly, although this has sometimes obliged the party to make some disconcerting *volte-face*.

It is not easy to explain in a few words the strength of the appeal of a totalitarian movement such as communism in so individualist and agricultural a country as France, particularly at a time when French citizens were being killed and wounded in the long and exhausting war against communist-led forces in Indo-China. It is essential, to begin with, to differentiate sharply between the active fraction of indoctrinated party members and the millions who simply vote for the communist party or follow communist directives in the trade unions. The history of the French communist party, and particularly the fluctuations in its membership, indicate that what attracts the French voter is primarily its class-conscious 'leftism', its claim to be the workers' party. A study of communist tactics since May 1947, when the party went into opposition, shows the extent to which it appeals to familiar left-wing attitudes and slogans—anti-clericalism, anti-colonialism, anti-fascism, anti-Vichy. The party itself is organized in such a way as to enable it to make the most of these popular appeals. Its tight structure of cells, sections, and federations, each responsible to and in contact only with the echelon above, and the rigid discipline imposed by the central committee, provide it with a unified and loyal personnel. It clearly has at its disposal considerable funds, enabling it to undertake, by press sales, mass meetings, and special organizations for women, youth, and so on, a far more intensive propaganda than any of the other parties can afford. Its leaders are, for the most part, pre-war veterans. M. Thorez, its secretary-general from 1932, has since 1950 been incapacitated through illness. The parliamentary leader, M. Duclos, was a foundation member of the party. Most of them are also of working-class origin, they live simply and spend their life in the service of the party as, indeed, do the active members at all levels.

All this, together with traditional trade union solidarity (and some communist pressure to maintain it) creates an appearance of dynamism and unity as against the more loosely organized democratic parties, which are internally disunited, disagree with each other and have, for the most part, leaders who are middle-class intellectuals. Marxist optimism—the sense of being on the side that history shows as bound to triumph—helps to maintain morale, as does the communist methods of 'self-criticism' which, by making individuals responsible for failures, creates the impression that the party is never wrong. The visibly shocking disparities between working-class standards of living and those of the so-called 'bourgeois' classes, and in particular the serious post-war housing situation, were real social grievances, and the isolation, the 'insularity' so to speak, of French small town and village life, enabled the communists to exploit, along with these grievances, local and sectional interests which are in reality often in conflict.

There are, however, at least three important weaknesses in communist propaganda. First, there is its blind support of Russia. The statement by Maurice Thorez in 1949 that France could not count on the workers in a war against Russia, created a real fear of a communist fifth column which has gone far to destroy the reputation for patriotism built up by the communists during the occupation. More important, two communist propaganda weapons—assumptions of the 'rightness' of the Soviet Union and of the existence of idyllic conditions in Soviet-dominated systems—were blunted with the suppression of the Hungarian revolution. For once, the communist press failed to insulate the French workers from the knowledge of what was happening, and controversies, misgivings and disillusionment were widespread in factories and in party organizations. Secondly, the average worker has grown weary of perpetual communist incitements to strike and is less and less willing to make the material sacrifices involved unless he can see some chance of immediate benefit.

The third weakness is one of internal organization. Self-criticism does not always function smoothly in a country whose press is free. When, in 1952, an old and tried leader, André Marty, was publicly disgraced, he reacted by refusing to admit his guilt and published his side of the case. The result was uneasiness among the communist supporters and some cracks in the façade of unity. It must be added, however, that the average worker's ignorance of any point of view other than that plugged by communists in press, factory and mine means that he is always better informed of the case *for* the party than of the case against it. And while the other parties fail to get rid of glaring social inequalities, the communists have always at their disposal the solid core of truth needed for the successful confusion of issues, characteristic of the party's propaganda.

The Socialists. If the strength of post-war communism is a complex phenomenon, the weakness of post-war socialism is a comparatively simple one. In spite of a comprehensive purge of those of its members guilty of collaboration with Vichy or the Germans during the war, the party was strong during the first year or two following the war and far more influential than its numbers would have led one to expect. Its leaders played an important part in the determination of post-war policy and in drawing up the text of the new constitution. The prestige of the party, and in particular, of its leader, Léon Blum, was such that, in December 1946, he was able to head an interim government composed wholly of socialists—a quite unprecedented event in French political history. The first President of the Fourth Republic, M. Vincent Auriol, was a socialist who had been President of the Constituent Assemblies and had been largely instrumental in bringing about sufficient agreement between the parties to enable them to agree on a constitutional text.

Yet between 1945 and 1951, the party lost votes steadily. In the elections of June 1951, the socialists polled only just over two and a half million votes, as against over four million in 1945. The circulation of the socialist daily, *Le Populaire*, which had been over a quarter of a million in the months following the liberation, was estimated to have fallen to about 30,000 in 1953. At one time a public subscription had to be launched to keep it alive. It should be added, however, that the party's strength had never lain in Paris, but rather in the industrial north-east and the rural areas of south and south-west France and that it had, and still has, an influential regional press, particularly in Lille, Marseilles and Limoges.

Members of the party explained these facts differently from many outsiders. Some outside observers attributed socialist success in the immediate post-war years less to the conversion of Frenchmen to socialism than to the temporary unpopularity of the other great republican and anti-clerical party, the radical party. They attributed the later decline of the socialist party to essentially the same causes as led to the decline of radicalism, namely, out-of-date modes of thought. In the words of one critic,

'The socialist party has followed the same evolution as the radical party at the beginning of the century, and has unconsciously taken its place; it has even inherited its doctrinal rigidity on anti-clericalism, a question which has for long been out-of-date.'[1]

Inside the party, the tendency was to attribute the decline to the compromises which socialists had to accept as the left wing of governmental coalitions, whilst their chief rivals for working-class support, the communists, being in opposition, were able, with total irresponsibility, to support popular claims. The slight socialist gains in the municipal elections in April 1953, when the party was once again in opposition, seemed to confirm this view and many socialists attributed the results directly to their decision (in February 1950, and from the beginning of the 1951 parliament) not to accept governmental office. In the 1956 elections, the Socialist party increased its vote by 450,000, partly, no doubt, as a result of its electorial alliance with the Radicals, then led by M. Mendès-France. Most of the increase was north of the Loire, and in regions where the communist party also increased its strength. Party membership (which was

[1] Jean Fabiani in *Combat*, 15.5.51.

over 300,000 in 1946) was, in 1958, about half that figure.

Socialist party organization is democratic. Policy decisions are taken by a *comité directeur* of thirty-one members (of whom ten may be members of parliament) elected directly at the annual congress. Delegates to the congress are chosen by the federations in the *départements*, and their votes reflect the strengths within each federation of the support given to two or three key resolutions. The federation groups the different local branches (*sections*) in the *département*. When decisions of particular importance are called for during the year, they are taken by the *Conseil National*, a kind of miniature congress, representative of all elements in the party, which meets at regular intervals and can be summoned to an extraordinary meeting if necessary.

The party has suffered from differences of opinion on a number of issues, on European integration, for example, and the rearmament of Germany, on what ought to be the party's relations with the communists or the MRP, on the policy which ought to be adopted in North Africa, on re-armament and the Indo-Chinese war. But once a question has been thrashed out in committee and a democratic vote taken, the party nearly always votes as one in the Assembly or the Council of the Republic. Indeed, it is the only democratic party which does so consistently.

On general principles, however, there is wholehearted agreement. In the economic and social field, the socialist party is in favour of public control of key industries, of planned production, and of price control if necessary, of social security and of a national minimum wage determined in relation to the cost of living. The 1951 election programme called specifically for reforms of the fiscal system to enable the state to rely more on income tax, instead of on taxes on consumption goods and on business transactions, both of which have repercussions on prices, for industrial re-equipment and controls aimed at bringing down prices, for the maintenance of the social security system and increased aid for families, old people and war victims. In the fields of overseas and foreign relations, it stressed socialist opposition to inequality and racial discrimination, and the need to seek opportunities of negotiation in the far East, it opposed German rearmament and reaffirmed socialist faith in collective security. From 1956 onwards, however, the party's policy on Algeria, while in office, though supported by a large majority of the rank and file, was increasingly unpopular with a small but influential minority.

In a new declaration of principles, drafted by Léon Blum after the war, the party also reaffirmed its fidelity to Marxism.

'The socialist party', it says, 'is essentially a revolutionary party and remains a party of class struggle.'

Anti-clericalism is an equally firm tenet. The party believes in a uniform system of state-controlled education and opposes all forms of aid for independent catholic schools.

To outside observers, the French socialist party's preoccupation with Marxism, or rather with interpretations of Marxism that accord with its own philosophy, has something both unreal and dilettante about it. Like its anti-clericalism, Marxism seems to be a doctrinal heritage rather than a living force and to hinder, instead of helping, the recruitment of new members. These doctrinal rigidities attract a high proportion of middle-class intellectuals, particularly teachers and civil servants, though they repel other intellectuals, and the party leadership seems to British eyes over-academic and out of contact with the day-to-day life of the workers. This impression is, of course, due in part to the organizational divorce between the party and the trade unions, partly, too, to the greater interest in all classes in theoretical and doctrinal questions than in the practical issues which dominate British political thinking. It is also explained to some extent by communist competition for working-class support, which keeps the party perpetually on the defensive against a rival which can represent itself as being more authentically Marxist.

Whatever may be the reasons, however, there is little doubt that one of the great weaknesses of the post-war party is that it no longer attracts working-class elements in sufficient numbers to prevent its opponents from classing it as a white-collar party. It includes more candidates and more members of parliament from the teaching profession than any other party. The 1951 Assembly included only three socialist deputies classed as 'workers' (as against thirty-three communist deputies so classed), but it included forty civil servants and members of the teaching profession, and thirty-one members of the liberal professions.[1] An analysis of the age and social position of local officials, published in a socialist periodical[2] in 1952, showed that the backbone of the party is composed of the older age groups and of professional and salaried classes. Of the members of departmental executive commissions, 70 per cent were over forty. Women played an infinitesimal role (only 5 per

---

[1] Figures included in the Ministry of the Interior's official election results (*La Documentation Française*, 1953), pp. 55–6.
[2] *Revue Socialiste*, March 1952.

cent) and those who did hold office were for the most part middle-aged or elderly. Over 60 per cent of the party officials of departmental executive commissions were wage or salary earners, but of these, only 13–14 per cent could be classed as 'workers'. Of the 526 socialist candidates in 1951, only 35 were classed as workers; of 542 communist candidates, 144 were classed as workers.

As the nearest neighbour of the communists, and for a long time the left wing of what was, in economic policy, a predominantly centre-right coalition, the socialists have had an uphill struggle since the war, in both the political and industrial fields. Their leaders have shown great courage and idealism in the most difficult circumstances. The firmness of M. Moch at the Interior was very largely responsible for the moderation and statesmanship with which the strikes were handled in 1948. M. Mollet has worked hard to try to reconcile the views of Great Britain and France on European integration. Socialist and socialistic trade union leaders have fought to keep the non-communist trade union elements from following the irresponsible lead of the CGT. Local parties have opposed communist tactics in local government. Although the socialist party has a great deal of lee-way to make up, from the end of 1953 it seemed to have turned the corner and to be not merely holding its own but actually gaining ground from the communists.

The MRP. Although undoubtedly the party closest to the socialists in its social, economic and international policy, the MRP has not yet succeeded in establishing itself firmly in French minds as an authentic left-wing party. Radicals and socialists alike regard it as a clerical party, and therefore with suspicion. Some of the radicals have been wary of its enthusiastic Europeanism as well, and both radicals and socialists, with their Jacobin and individualist heritage, find MRP pluralism, the insistence on the value of social units, in particular, of the family, an alien concept which they suspect of being used to serve catholic rather than socialist or progressive ends.

'The true design of the democracies to come is pluralism,' said M. Teitgen, at the time of the constitutional debates, '. . . in France, there are diverse spiritual families; it is not by suppressing this diversity that you will create national unanimity; on the contrary, you can do this by giving them the means of their development.'[1]

If the average anti-clerical socialist or radical were to be asked what he took this to mean in terms of practical policy, he would no doubt reply that it would certainly be used as a defence of the existing school system in Alsace-Lorraine. This has long offended both the anti-clericalism and the passion for uniformity which distinguish the French Left.

On the other hand, some of those who supported the MRP did so because it was an anti-Marxist party and because it included during the immediate post-war years a considerable Gaullist element; these were suspicious of its emphasis on economic democracy as an essential concomitant of political democracy and of its belief in trade-unionism and its general championship of the workers.

The MRP thus fell between two stools. Or rather, to be more precise, it first rose and then fell because of this diversity of appeal. In 1946, five and a half million people voted for the MRP and the MRP group in

[1] Einaudi and Goguel, *Christian Democracy in Italy and France* (University of Notre Dame Press, 1952), p. 137.

the Assembly numbered over 160 deputies. With the recovery of the conservative parties and the growth of General de Gaulle's Rally, however, its strength declined and, in 1951, it obtained only two and a half million votes and constituted the smallest of the six major groupings in the Assembly.[1] None of the lost ground was regained in 1956. This change of fortune confirmed the opinion of many Frenchmen that the success of the MRP in the immediate post-war years was to be attributed more to the discredit of the orthodox right-wing parties and to the MRP's lack of a political past, than to the inherent attractiveness of MRP doctrine. It left the party more homogeneous, both leadership and rank and file being, now, as the leaders had been in the main all along, economically and socially to the left of the radicals. It is symptomatic of French traditionalism in politics that it continues to sit on the right of the radicals in the Assembly, the latter, as an anti-clerical party, having an undisputed claim to be regarded as being on the Left.

The MRP is regarded as being the party *par excellence* of the Fourth Republic, as the radical party was of the Third. And more than any other party the MRP has been associated in French minds with the post-war policy of European integration, within a framework of supra-national institutions. The party's fortunes have, therefore, tended to fluctuate with the success or failure of plans for further European integration. The MRP has suffered too, at times, as has the socialist party from the unpopularity involved in constituting the left-wing element of coalitions with right-wing parties.

[1] That is, if the radicals and UDSR are treated as a single grouping.

The main electoral strength of the MRP lies in the strongly catholic *départements* of east and west France. The party also attracts a number of non-catholic votes and has always endeavoured not to be classed as a purely catholic party. Its appeal is really threefold. First, in a country in which political scandals have at one time or another involved members of most of the traditional parties, in which memories of war-time collaboration with the enemy (which leave no pre-war party entirely unscathed) die hard, and in which the prestige of politics and politicians is generally low, the MRP stands out as a party which not merely emphasizes moral and spiritual values but also, being new, has itself a clean slate. Its reputation for integrity, its resistance record, its insistence on the value of a healthy family life, its international idealism, have all helped to attract a clientele among young people hoping for a post-war French moral renaissance as well as among the a-political, or among those who are cynical or disgusted with party politics. Secondly it is a relatively united party, because its general philosophy is that of progressive catholicism everywhere. And thirdly, its economic and social policy, its contacts with the catholic trade union movement give it a solid organization. The party gives the impression of having its feet on the ground; it is a disciplined national party with democratically organized institutions. These are characteristics which previously belonged only to the socialists and communists.

The weakness of the MRP lies partly in the relative political inexperience of its leaders, whose approach to constitutional and European questions in particular tends to be over-academic and theoretical, and partly in its inability to make sufficient impact in non-catholic circles, especially in rural areas and in local government.

This is perhaps less a failure on the part of the MRP than a result of causes largely outside its control. The strong sense of political tradition on the Left means that any new party is faced with an uphill struggle. The MRP's central position in the post-war party structure makes its support essential to almost any viable governmental coalition. The communists are in permanent opposition, and so, whenever the socialists are also in opposition, it inevitably constitutes a small left-wing minority in a predominantly right-wing coalition. This was the position of the socialists up to 1951 and is what more than anything else led them to move into opposition. The MRP inherited this unenviable position, which strengthens the instinctive conviction of the left-wing villager that a party approved by the Pope and supported by the *curé* must of necessity be reactionary. It will take more than a decade to break down this suspicion and the concentration of MRP votes in predominantly catholic and conservative regions does not help to weaken it. On the other hand, Frenchmen with progressive social or economic policies, who would like to see reforms similar to those introduced by the British Labour Party, but who cannot subscribe to the 'Marxist' inspiration and vocabulary of the socialist party, are driven in post-war France to support the MRP, because the radical party, though still republican and anti-clerical, is no longer in sympathy with left-wing social and economic policies.

The MRP has under 100,000 members[1] and is organized democratically in local sections and departmental federations. It holds an annual congress. Its organization differs from that of the socialist party in attaching less importance in congresses to a strictly proportional representation of

[1] In 1947 M. Fauvet estimated its membership at 450,000.

rank and file opinion and in attaching more weight in executive bodies to the representation of parliamentary leaders (of whom the socialist rank and file is always deeply distrustful). It also attaches great importance to the organization of specialized study groups. Indeed, this tendency was already evident even in the resistance formations which formed the nucleus of the post-war party.

In spite of its reduction in numbers since 1946, the party has considerable prestige, particularly in the field of foreign affairs. Except for the month of December 1946, when M. Blum's interim socialist government was in office, either M. Bidault or M. Schuman was at the Ministry of Foreign Affairs from 1944 to June 1954. The party's influence in the press has declined, the one MRP Paris daily (*L'Aube*), which, in 1946, had a circulation of nearly a quarter of a million, having ceased publication in 1951. Two important provincial papers, however, *Ouest-France* and *Nord-Eclair* are politically in sympathy with the MRP and, like the socialist party, the MRP has a number of periodicals destined for internal consumption.

The Radicals and the UDSR. From the radical party rightwards, the structure of French parties changes. The three left-wing parties already described are highly organized, with regular contacts between the leadership and the rank and file. Both socialists and communists have disciplined parliamentary groups. The MRP vote is more liable to be divided, but the radical party is regularly divided. The party is not only itself more loosely organized but has been subject in the 1951 and 1956 Assemblies to a number of internal divisions. It has been traditionally allied, with a number of small groups, to form the RGR (*Rassemblement des Gauches*

6

Républicaines), a coalition whose character and organization it has never been easy to define with any degree of precision.

As such, it had no individual members, being a federation existing essentially for purposes of information and electoral association. At the 1956 election, however, M. Edgar Faure and a number of his fellow-radicals, expelled with him from the radical party at the time of the dissolution, took the title of RGR, and this title was retained by the group of some 14 members of which he was the leader in the Assembly. Differences between it and the orthodox radical party were personal rather than political. In October 1956 another small group of 'dissident radicals' was formed,[1] also numbering about 14 deputies, including two former Prime Ministers, MM. Queuille and Marie. It was somewhat to the right of the RGR group, but shared its dislike of M. Mendès-France. At the beginning of 1958 there were attempts at a reunification, possibly including the other near-radical formation, the UDSR, and some of the orthodox radicals.

The UDSR began as a post-war resistance movement, with socialist sympathies, and at first included a number of loyal supporters of General de Gaulle, who, later, joined the RPF. Though a small parliamentary group, it is important. It now includes a high proportion of overseas deputies and since 1956 has been allied in the Assembly with a small overseas group, the *Rassemblement Démocratique Africain*. It has some local organizations, but is strong in only a dozen or so *départements*.

RGR, 'Dissidents', UDSR, and the so-called 'orthodox'

[1] In January 1958, the group adopted the traditional radical title of *Parti de la Gauche démocratique et radical-socialiste*.

radicals all constitute different aspects of radicalism, which has always included a number of differing shades of opinion. Since the war, however, the party has, in general, been much closer to the Right in the economic field that it was before the war. As M. Goguel puts it: 'as they have hardly changed at all, while everything around has changed, they have ended up as a socially conservative party. . . .'[1]

The social conservatism and parliamentary indiscipline of radicals were the chief targets of M. Mendès-France during the two years, from May 1955, during which, with the retirement of M. Herriot from the presidency, he became the effective leader of the radical party. The constitution was revised, and attempts were made to give the party a programme and to oblige the parliamentary group to obey the party whip. The attempts failed, and, in May 1957, M. Mendès-France resigned from the leadership, only a small following of a dozen or so deputies remaining loyal to him in the Assembly. The radical party remains, therefore, what it has always been, and there is every reason to suppose that the party organization, too, will revert to its traditional forms, of which a brief account ought perhaps to be given.

The orthodox radical party, entitled the Radical Republican and Socialist Radical party, is the oldest of all French parties, having been founded in 1901. Its membership cannot be accurately assessed because the local organizations are very independent, local personalities play an important role and electoral alliances with widely varying local bases are common. The party's postwar fortunes have fluctuated. As the most important party of the Third Republic, the governmental

[1] *Foreign Affairs*, Oct. 1954, p. 113.

party *par excellence*, the radical party was associated in French minds at the end of the war with all that they disliked in pre-war French politics. The attachment of post-war radicals to the constitution of the then discredited régime, their bitter and highly vocal opposition to the innovations favoured by the other left-wing parties, in particular their dislike of the nationalization measures passed by the provisional government—all this did nothing to increase their popularity. In October 1945, the radicals polled a million and three-quarter votes and had only twenty-nine representatives in the Assembly. Gradually, their influence in the Assembly increased and their standing in the country improved. In 1946 and 1951, the radical (including UDSR) vote was in the region of two and a quarter million.[1] In 1956, when Radicals (and some UDSR) formed an electoral alliance with the Socialists, it increased by half a million. The main strength of radicalism is in central and south-west France, essentially a region of small towns, small farms and a small-town, economically conservative mentality.

Radical party membership is small, in the neighbourhood of 50,000 only. Party organization is at the same time complex and diffuse. The local *comités* have a great deal of autonomy. There is the usual framework of local sections and departmental federations, the latter sending delegates to an annual congress. But resemblance to socialist and MRP organizations stops there. Voting at the congress is not restricted to mandated delegates and so is not representative of rank and file opinion, but

[1] It is always difficult to estimate accurately the radical vote. In 1946 there were no radical candidates in twenty-one constituencies where radical candidates had polled over 200,000 votes in the June elections of that year. In 1951 and 1956 there were varying coalitions between radicals and other parties.

of whatever members turn up. The relation to each other and to rank and file opinion of the three executive bodies is not easy to describe. The executive commission of seventy is elected by the congress and meets regularly. The executive committee is very large indeed—between one and two thousand—and includes along with a number of elected members, radical deputies, *Conseillers généraux* and some municipal councillors. It meets every quarter as a kind of miniature congress, but is rendered unrepresentative by an inevitably high proportion of absenteeism, a low quorum, and by the consequent possibility of packing. The *Comité Cadillac*, which includes both members of the executive commission and of the radical parliamentary group, meets only intermittently. It is the body, however, that is responsible for immediate policy decisions at times of governmental crisis. The effective leadership of the party belongs to none of these organs, but to

'small groups of leading personalities, constituting coteries whose rivalry or coalitions in the last analysis determine policy'.[1]

The radical party is, thus, at its centre a kind of camouflaged oligarchy, and at its extremities a collection of more or less autonomous federations.

In the eve-of-war Chamber of Deputies, the radical party constituted the second largest group. Of the six major political tendencies represented in the first post-war National Assembly, radicals and UDSR together were the weakest, and in the second, were only slightly stronger than the MRP. If the French voter is tending to move away from radicalism, thus continuing a tendency

[1] Goguel, 'Les Partis Politiques en France' (*Encyclopédie Politique, I*), p. 324.

already evident before the war, radicalism nevertheless remains an important force in French political life. The radical party has been called the party of Presidents. From 1947 to the end of 1953, both Assemblies were presided over by radicals. In periods of crisis, there is a noticeable tendency for parliament to fall back on a radical leader and, of the twenty-two governments which held office from the resignation of General de Gaulle in January 1946 to the end of 1957, ten were headed by radical Prime Ministers. Most of the post-war radical leaders were already parliamentary figures before the war; M. Herriot, for long President of the party and also President of both the pre-war Chamber of Deputies and the National Assembly; M. Daladier, the President of the RGR, M. Queuille, M. André Marie, M. Mendès-France were all members of the pre-war *Chambre des Députés*. The post-war party had a left wing of young and rising politicians which was depleted in 1946 by the defection of some half dozen, several of whom—the best-known being M. Pierre Cot—joined the small fellow-travelling group in the Assembly, the *Républicains Progressistes*. The party includes, however, a number of younger leaders who are coming more and more to the fore. They include, for instance, M. Edgar Faure, who, at forty-three was, for a month in 1952, France's youngest Prime Minister, M. Mendès-France, who, at forty-seven, became Prime Minister in June 1954, M. Bourgés-Maunoury and M. Félix Gaillard, who both established new records as the Fourth Republic's youngest Prime Ministers.

The party's parliamentary strength derives in the main from its traditional reputation for providing statesmen, from its central position in the Assembly, and from its importance in local affairs, which gives it a predominant position in the Council of the Republic. Today, even more than before the war, radicalism represents either concrete interests, often specific local interests, or a general temperament, a state of mind, but it has no definite programme or doctrine. There is, indeed, a wide range of opinion within the party. There is a conservatism barely distinguishable from that of the Right, with which local radical parties often conclude electoral alliances; there is the traditional republican anti-clerical individualism of elder statesmen like M. Daladier and M. Queuille; and there is the belief in economic planning and tax reform, though falling short of socialism, characteristic of younger men like M. Mendès-France and M. Edgar Faure. It is not surprising that, of all political parties, the radicals are most frequently divided on important issues into three distinct—and often almost equal—sections.

If it is not easy to say precisely what radicalism stands for, it is relatively easy to understand why, in spite of the party's post-war conservatism in economic matters, it is still classed in the minds of the majority of Frenchmen as a party of the Left. Politically, it is one of the heirs of the Revolution; its republicanism is no less, and its anti-clericalism is scarcely less wholehearted than are those sentiments among members of the socialist and communist parties. Its 'leftness' is, therefore, in the mind of the French elector, a tradition strong enough to make him forget, or at least overlook, its increasing economic traditionalism.

The Orthodox Right. The Right is composed, as it was in pre-war France, of a number of small groups, whose membership and names change frequently. They retain, however, through all their transformations, certain family resemblances. As in pre-war France, right-wing groups still refuse to describe themselves as 'conservative'; *'modéré'*, *'action sociale'*, *'paysan'*, *'républicain'*, *'indépendant'*, used singly or in combinations are all recognized right-wing labels. One of the groups in the 1946 Assembly succeeded in combining nearly all of these by calling itself the *Centre Républicain Indépendant d'Action Paysanne et Sociale*. The 1956 Assembly included two main conservative groups, the *Indépendants*, whose full title was, in 1958, the *Groupe des Indépendants et Paysans d'Action Sociale*, numbering, with a small associated group, some ninety deputies; and a small Peasant group of about a dozen deputies. The composition of groups calling themselves 'peasant'—in fact few, if any, of their members have even a remote connexion with the peasantry—is highly variable, and there have been four or five groups since the war, whose nomenclature has changed more than their policy.[1] Movement from one conservative group to another is common; groups are often ephemeral, and it is doubtful whether their own members are always clear as to what distinguishes one from another. In 1945, the *Parti Républicain de la Liberté* was founded with the intention of making it into a strong conservative party. The attempt failed, as previous attempts had done, owing to the high degree of individualism which has always characterised conservative organizations in France. From 1949 onwards, the *Centre National des Indépendants* has constituted a loosely organized co-ordinating body for conservative groups, but it is not responsible for the determination of policy and has no real control over right-wing deputies. Nor is there any unified organization in the country.

[1] See Appendix 3 showing changes in groups from 1951 onwards.

Right-wing groups exhibit a great variety of opinions, ranging from narrow and sectional reaction (the Peasant group was associated from 1957 onwards with the Poujadists) to the moderate conservatism of men like M. Reynaud, or M. Pinay. Though there is no such thing as a conservative policy, it is possible to sum up briefly the general preoccupations of conservatives as being in the main:

(i) support for the interests of the small producer, opposition to State controls (except when in the interests of producers), opposition to increased taxation, or to fiscal reform, and also to extensions of the social services,

(ii) the defence of the French Union, by which is meant, opposition to nationalist movements in overseas territories and sympathy with the point of view of the European residents in Algeria,

(iii) the defence of Catholic claims in the sphere of education.

They have divided views regarding projects for European integration.

The main strength of the Right is in the rural areas of central and eastern France, the formerly conservative regions of western France having been partially captured by the MRP and the RPF. Right-wing organizations in the country are numerous and decentralized.

The Unorthodox Right. Although RPF deputies in the 1951 Assembly sat, much against their will, on the extreme right of the Assembly, the leaders of the movement always denied that it was conservative. It was founded by General de Gaulle in April 1947 and its main appeal, as is indicated by its title, the French People's Rally (*Le Rassemblement du Peuple Français*, or RPF), was its insistence on the need for French unity under the leadership of General de Gaulle. It attracted many of those French citizens who were disillusioned by the dissensions between the political parties and disturbed by the consequent weakness and instability of French governments, as well as those who saw the communist strength in the Assembly and the trade unions a threat both to parliamentary government and to industrial recovery. The movement contained, however, from the beginning, internal contradictions or ambiguities which were not apparent while it remained, as it did from 1947 to 1951, an extra-parliamentary organization, whose supporters in the Assembly had been elected under other labels and were only 'unofficial' supporters of General de Gaulle's ideas.

During this period, the movement served in the main to mobilize political discontent. General de Gaulle held the view that the régime was rotting away and his supporters could, therefore, look forward to his assumption of power in a short time, when the inevitable collapse occurred. By 1951, however, this attitude was less tenable. The break-up of the régime seemed as far away as ever, the communist threat was somewhat less serious then it had appeared in 1947, and the international situation was, in the opinion of many Frenchmen who were in general sympathy with Gaullism, too serious to justify what the General's opponents called *la politique du pire*, that is a policy of waiting for—if not hoping for—disaster. Moreover, the movement had grown rapidly and could confidently hope to be the largest group in the next Assembly, if it were to follow the normal constitutional route to power.

The RPF, therefore, contested the 1951 elections as a political party. In spite of an electoral system designed to minimize its representation (along with that of the communists) some four million electors voted for Gaullist candidates and the RPF constituted the largest group in the Assembly. Yet, in less than a year, the Gaullist movement had begun to disintegrate and by May 1953 General de Gaulle had publicly washed his hands of its parliamentary representatives.

The position of the RPF as one of the several parliamentary parties, but without a clear majority of its own, was much more difficult than it had been when the movement was an extra-parliamentary *Rassemblement*. Deputies could not remain in the position of irresponsible onlookers. They were obliged to vote for or against concrete proposals. If they remained in permanent opposition, an attitude consistent with their previous attitude to the régime, they not only laid themselves open to the criticism of pursuing *la politique du pire*, but they found themselves in permanent alliance with their chief enemies, the communists. If, on the other hand, they voted for measures that were in the main in accordance with their own ideas, there was bound to come a time when they would have to consider the possibility of accepting governmental responsibilities. They were too large a party to escape these responsibilities, but not large enough to change the constitution and bring General de Gaulle to power, as they had hoped to do.

The crisis came in 1952. Since 1947, the right-wing parties had been growing steadily stronger, and in 1952, M. Pinay, a leader of the *Républicains Indépendants*, was asked to form a government. To some of those who, in 1947, had seen in Gaullism the main defence against communism, there now existed an alternative which had the added attraction of offering the prospect of political office. Thirty-two members of the RPF, most of them belonging to the conservative wing and a number of them pre-war conservative politicians, decided to support M. Pinay. They were expelled from the movement by General de Gaulle in the following July and from then on formed an independent parliamentary group, called the *Action Républicaine et Sociale* (ARS). The municipal elections in the following spring showed a distinct swing of opinion against the RPF and in favour of M. Pinay's group. As was only natural, some Gaullist deputies and municipal councillors, who were not indifferent to the prospects of re-election, began to seek alliances with the orthodox conservative groups. General de Gaulle's reaction to this situation was to announce on 6 May that the French People's Rally would no longer associate itself with parliamentary action. The eighty-odd RPF deputies were, therefore, left without a leader and, since the movement's inspiration and rallying point had been the leadership of General de Gaulle, without any real *raison d'être*. Most of them decided to remain united in a parliamentary group and they adopted, at first, the title of *Union Républicaine et d'Action Sociale* (URAS). Later, they came to be known as *Républicains Sociaux*.

In the 1956 elections the Social Republicans obtained under a million votes and their small group of twenty-one members was distinguished from other moderate right-wing parties only by its insistence on the need for a new constitution of the Presidential type, and for its growing belief in some form of federal relationship (not clearly defined) between France and the North African territories.

The original Gaullist function of mobilising discontent was taken on, from 1953 onwards, by the movement known as Poujadist, but which began in 1953 as a small sectional pressure group, the *Union de Défense des Commerçants et Artisans* founded by M. Pierre Poujade in south-west France. The movement represented small shopkeepers, and, in particular, those, often uneconomic family businesses that were beginning to feel the pinch of competition from larger and more modern concerns (particularly co-operatives), and also the pinch of fiscal pressure, owing both to the stabilisation of prices and to the tightening-up of tax collection, carried out by M. Edgar Faure at the Ministry of Finance. It was a revolt, both against the methods of tax collection, which were often a burden to the little man, obliged to act as a tax collector, and usually ill-equipped to do so, and against the tax inspector, whose greater efficiency was depriving the small man of what at times was his only method of making ends meet, namely, tax evasion.

From 1953 to 1955, there was growing public disillusionment with the functioning of parliamentary institutions. These were the years of controversy over E.D.C., of stalemate in North Africa, and of abortive discussions in the Assembly on electoral reform, ending in the defeat of the government, dissolution and a general election. M. Poujade was enabled during these years not only to extend his organization but to widen the scope of its appeal, and, by 1955, could attract audiences of some thousands to mass meetings which he held up and down the country. A natural demogogic orator of some talent, he appealed primarily to the fears and xenophobia of the little man, in fact to precisely those elements that, in the 'thirties, had been susceptible to fascist propaganda. And there were in Poujadist propaganda, too, disquieting elements of anti-semitism, of anti-parliamentarism, and hints of violence. The two and a half million votes obtained by the Poujadist lists in the 1956 elections were by no means restricted to the south-west. In thirty-three *départements*, Poujadist candidates received over 15 per cent of the votes cast (in one, over 25 per cent), a record surpassed only by the socialist and communist parties. What these electors were voting for was far from clear, for, except for the demand for the calling of a States-General, representing the professions, the Poujadist programme has no positive content. Nor had this item been worked out in any detail. The basis of representation, the methods of convening such a body, what it was to do, all this was left in the air.

Neither in the Assembly, nor in the country, however, did the movement make much impact during the following two years. A number of internal dissensions, together with some alleged financial irregularities, certainly helped to weaken the organization in the country. In the Assembly, the group, reduced, by 1958, to some thirty deputies, merely constituted an uninfluential body of uncomprehending and unassimilable small-town reactionaries, inclined to hooliganism.

The Trade Unions. Since the Amiens congress of 1906, the trade union movement in France has been by tradition independent of all political parties. With the formation of the communist party, however, in 1921, after the schism of Tours, this theory became, for considerable numbers of trade unionists, no more than a convenient fiction. The communist and non-communist wings of the movement (CGTU and CGT) remained apart until 1936 and separated again in 1939, after the signature of the Russo-German Pact. During the occupation, the underground resistance movement decided to reunite and the unity of the two movements was ratified in 1945. Duality at every organizational level was retained, as in the period 1936–9, and for two years, there was, therefore, increasing friction between communist and non-communist officials.

At the end of 1947, as a result of the communist-inspired strikes of that autumn, the non-communist elements set up an independent organization, the *Confédération Générale du Travail—Force Ouvrière* (CGT—FO).[1] The bulk of the membership remained, however, within the parent organization, the CGT, which retained the headquarters and the official journal, *Le Peuple*. Today, therefore, three-quarters of the organized workers are included in this now communist-dominated organization. While this means, of course, that the leaders are working hand in hand with the communist party, it does not mean that they can always count on the rank and file to obey communist directives unquestionably. Many of the members are trade unionists first and communists second—or not at all—and communist attempts to declare strikes have at times met with only half-hearted responses where the pretext was clearly political.

Non-communist trade unionism is divided into three main bodies and several smaller organizations. There is the catholic confederation (*la Confédération Française des Travailleurs Chrétiens*, or CFTC) which already had its own independent organization from the end of the First World War and has never consented to fusion

---

[1] The journal *Force Ouvrière* was founded in December 1945, as the descendant of the underground trade union paper *Résistance Ouvrière*. It openly resisted communist attempts at 'colonizàtion', which was even then seen to constitute a danger to the movement.

with the main trade union movement; there is the *Force Ouvrière* confederation, set up in 1947; and there is the organization for overseers and technical staffs (*Confédération Générale des Cadres*, or CGC), claiming in 1946 to include some 80,000 members and 100,000 the following year. There are also three smaller movements. There is the National Confederation of Labour (*Confédération Nationale du Travail*), a small group of anarcho-syndicalist tendencies, created in May 1946 as a reaction against the communist domination of the CGT which the congress of the previous month had revealed. There is the Confederation of Independent Workers (*Confédération des Travailleurs Indépendants*), formed in 1949 and including several heterogeneous elements, from supporters of the pre-war tendency, represented in the journal *Syndicats* (leader, René Belin) many of whose members collaborated with the Vichy régime, to former communists who had opposed the Russo-German Pact, and even to supporters of the RPF. It, too, is numerically very small. The third, even smaller, though more influential, is the Federation of Autonomous Unions. It was formed before the split between the CGT and the CGT–FO but was joined in 1947 by unions representing the teaching profession.

All these adhere to the traditional non-political policy of French trade unionism. Their membership, all told, cannot amount to as much as two million and their opponents would put the figure a great deal lower. In 1952, the Secretary-General of CGT–FO gave its membership as 1,120,000. CFTC membership is probably about half a million, and the three small confederations are not likely to have more than a quarter of a million members. The CGC, which claimed to have a membership of 120,000 in 1952, is not, of course, a workers' organization. In a similar category is the General Confederation of Agriculture (CGA), a post-war organization, grouping in the main peasant farmers.[1] The communist-dominated movement, though much the largest, lost ground with the coming of economic prosperity in 1954–6, and again after the Hungarian revolution. In 1946, at the peak period of trade union membership, the united CGT movement had an estimated membership of over six millions. Since 1947, the two main movements have both complained of apathy in the ranks, of unpaid subscriptions and unattended branch and general meetings. It is doubtful, therefore, whether in the 'fifties membership even reached half the 1946 figure.

Trade union organization is both vertical and regional. The different industries are grouped in national federations, of which there are, in the CGT and CGT—FO about thirty-five to forty, some of them very small. In 1946, just before the split, the jewellery workers' federation, for instance, had 8,000 and the commercial travellers' federation 15,000 members. Half a dozen federations had over 300,000 members, the largest, the metal-workers' having 900,000, the others, all with memberships of between 300,000 and 400,000, being the railway workers', the building trade workers', and the miners'. There are also departmental and inter-departmental federations. In the united movement, national and regional federations sent delegates to the national confederal committee (CCN) which was the responsible body between congresses. These were held biennially, the first and only united congress to be held since

[1] There is an organization grouping agricultural workers, the *Fédération des Travailleurs Agricoles*, but it is, of course, affiliated to the CGT. It is numerically far less important, with some 200,000 members at most at the peak period of 1946.

7

1938 being that of 1946. The CFTC has an annual congress.

It cannot be denied that non-communist trade unionism is weak as well as disunited. Many explanations have been put forward to explain the continued predominance of the communist-dominated movement. The combination of communist unity and drive (on the part of the leaders, that is) and non-communist disunity and rank and file apathy has been an important factor. The ruthless exploitation by the communists of their familiar tactics of infiltration during the years of so-called unity also enabled them to get a grip on the movement which was a great help to them when the split came. The non-communist elements had genuinely desired to create a strong and united movement and had leaned over backwards in their efforts to be fair to the communists and to let bygones be bygones. Their goodwill was, naturally, unscrupulously abused by the communists, who had already largely succeeded in capturing the key positions before the 1946 congress.[1]

A number of other factors helped to weaken the position of the non-communists at this stage—the absence of Léon Jouhaux, for instance, during the first months of reconstitution of the unions after the war, which enabled the communists to obtain a *de facto* majority on the executive from the start; the loss of some able leaders, such as MM. Lacoste, Pineau and Gazier, who chose political careers as socialist deputies; the depletion of non-communist elements, owing to the purge of collaborators, which, of course, left communist effectives untouched, as the party had already gone underground

[1] Of the thirty-five seats on the administrative commission, twenty went to the communists.

before the capitulation. When the split came there were obvious reasons why the CGT should remain the stronger—the solidarity of the working class, to whom the familiar name, headquarters and trade union journal were in themselves strong appeals to loyalty; the greater propagandist opportunities of the CGT, thanks to its retention of the funds of the movement. As against this combination of advantages, the much smaller CGT–FO, at first without premises and almost without funds, was faced with the tremendous task of building a new organization and endeavouring, in difficult circumstances, to appeal to the reason and sense of responsibility of its members, where its rivals were animated by no such scruples.

The Employers' Organizations. Like the pre-war trade union confederations, the pre-war employers' organizations were dissolved after the capitulation. After the war, a new organization, the National Council of French Employers (*Conseil National du Patronat Français*, or CNPF) was created at the beginning of 1946. It is organized in vertical federations of industries and trades and in inter-occupational regional federations. Its purpose is to represent and to co-ordinate employing interests in general. It includes as a constituent, autonomous organization, the general confederation of small and medium-sized undertakings (*Confédération Générale des Petites et Moyennes Entreprises*). The CNPF, however, represents predominantly large-scale industry, since seats on the governing body, the general Assembly, are allotted between member organizations in proportion to the number of wage-earners employed. Thus, over half its membership consists of the industrial federations. The CNPF can co-opt members of organizations, such as the Young Employers' Centre.

It maintains contacts with chambers of commerce and agriculture and with trade chambers.

French and British party systems. This summary of the organization and outlook of French post-war parties and trade unions, although necessarily incomplete, is nevertheless sufficient to throw into clear relief a number of obvious differences between the French and British party systems. There are many more parties in France, and with less stable membership, and they disagree on fundamentals as well as on matters of immediate policy. At the end of the war, many Frenchmen hoped that at least there would not be added to France's many material and psychological difficulties the kind of challenge to the régime that had existed in the thirties. They were destined to be disappointed. And even the parties which, from 1947 onwards, were compelled to try to work together as governmental parties were divided on most of the questions of immediate policy.

French parties also differ over a wider range of subjects. Catholic education, the electoral system, constitutional questions and matters of parliamentary procedure are only rarely matters of dispute in Great Britain. But since the war, the French parliament has discussed these questions, if not at greater length, certainly with more passion than it has lavished on any other subject, not excluding the cost of living. It may be objected that the circumstances were exceptional, that it is not every few years, even in France, that a new constitution is drawn up, that radical changes had also been made in the political and economic system, so that there were bound to be a number of questions left over for discussion. But such discussions were also characteristic of pre-war France. Between the wars, French deputies argued about the electoral system in 1919, 1924, 1927 and again in 1939, only a few weeks before the outbreak of war; they were concerned about the powers of the executive in 1934, and about the role of the Senate in 1937 and 1938. There were heated discussions in 1928 and 1930 about the survival of denominational education in Alsace-Lorraine and the growth of separatism in these three *départements*. Since the war, the question which, more than any other, has created bad feeling between the socialists and the MRP is that of financial support for catholic education. The merits and demerits of rival electoral systems were debated by the French Assembly on and off from January to May 1951, and again, for five weeks, in 1955, and yet again in 1958.

Membership of French parliamentary groups is relatively fluid and, as has been said, movement from one to the other is frequent. This general statement should, however, be qualified in several ways. First, the number of individuals who do change their party is only a small proportion of the total and those who make a habit of it can be almost counted on the fingers of one hand. M. Lécrivain-Servoz, elected for the Rhône in 1946 as a member of the MRP, subsequently became a member of the *Union Démocratique des Indépendants* (UDI), the *Action Républicaine et Sociale*, and, at the beginning of 1950, joined the group of coloured deputies from overseas, the *Indépendants d'Outre-Mer*. At the end of the parliament he was administratively attached to the small fellow-travelling group, the *Union des Républicains Progressistes* (URP) and he presented himself for re-election on a list entitled *Union pour l'Indépendance Française*. Comprehensibly in the circumstances, he was not re-elected. M. Raulin-Laboureur, elected in 1945 as a member of the socialistic *Groupe de la Résistance*

Démocratique et Sociale (afterwards the UDSR), sat for the Seine in 1946, being elected under the label *Union contre le tripartisme*. By the end of the Parliament he belonged to no group (*Non-inscrit*), but had been for a time a member both of the UDSR and the RPF. He was not re-elected in 1951, but by October of that year was contesting a by-election in the Ille et Vilaine as an *Indépendant*, that is, a conservative. Both these cases are exceptional and both concern deputies who were not re-elected after their extensive parliamentary travels. The few deputies who do change their group generally join one of a not dissimilar political colouring, or become independents, or else attach themselves as *apparentés*[1] to some group for purposes of convenience, because participation in the work of the parliamentary Commissions is restricted to members of organized groups numbering not less than 28 deputies, including *apparentés* (14 up to October 1958). Sometimes the change is the result of a temporary disagreement with their group and, after a short time, they return to it.

Another factor that makes group fluidity less important than it sometimes appears is the relatively high proportion of overseas deputies among those who change their groups. It must not be forgotten that 82 of France's 626 deputies are elected by overseas constituencies. Some 50 of them are coloured, many with only recently acquired political experience and with less interest in the affairs of France than in those that concern their own countries. It is natural that their attachment to French political parties should be less close than that of Frenchmen. Many of them join specifically overseas

---

[1] Not to be confused with the same word, used in connexion with the 1951 electoral law, with a quite different meaning.

groups—the *Convention Africaine* (formally IOM) or the RDA; others are loosely attached to other groups as *apparentés*. For example in the 1951 Parliament, of the 20 coloured representatives of West Africa, 9 were members of the IOM and 5 were *apparentés* to other groups. Of the 15 members elected for the Algerian second (that is, native) college, 8 were *apparentés*.

One characteristic which groups have in common is their relative indifference, as compared with British parties, to concrete programmes. For instance, the political declarations submitted by each parliamentary group (in accordance with the Assembly's standing orders) to the *Bureau* of the Assembly at the beginning of the new parliament in 1951 consist either of general statements of objectives, such as the 'construction of a just and fraternal Republic', 'the healthy management of public affairs, social peace and justice and the defence of liberty', 'the defence of national independence and international co-operation for peace', or else they list the measures that each party would like to see introduced, leaving out of account the obstacle of their mutual incompatibility.

This procedure is less unrealistic than it might appear. Since French governments are invariably coalitions of three or more parties, programmes and election manifestoes on the model of those of British parties would be useless. No party can undertake to do anything, because the terms on which it becomes a partner in the government have to be worked out painfully after the election. In these circumstances the party tends to base its appeal on its general philosophy and on one or two concrete proposals or issues of local interest to which special importance is attached.

It is not always helpful or relevant to press too far

comparisons and contrasts between British and French party politics. For parties, like any other spontaneous national grouping, are inevitably coloured by the national heritage and the national temperament. They are parts of the political whole and can only be properly understood as such.

CHAPTER V

THE ADMINISTRATIVE AND JUDICIAL FRAMEWORK

FRENCH administration is both rigid and highly centralized. It consists essentially of four organs: (1) the central government departments, together with their branches in the *départements*, working with, and partly under the direction of, the prefect; (2) the local government authorities, closely supervised by the Ministry of the Interior, or his agent in the *département*, the prefect; (3) the partially autonomous bodies, such as the nationalized industries, the social security services, and so on; and (4) the supervisory bodies, headed by the *Cour des Comptes* and the *Conseil d'Etat*.

(a) THE GOVERNMENT DEPARTMENTS

Since the war, most governments have included four categories of minister—Deputy Prime Ministers, Ministers of State, Ministers and Secretaries of State. Ministers of State are usually, though not always, without portfolio and may or may not be also Deputy Prime Ministers. Thus, in M. Pinay's government, in 1952, M. Queuille was both Deputy Prime Minister and Minister of State without portfolio; while in M. Laniel's government in 1953 there were three Deputy Prime Ministers, all without portfolio, one Minister of State with, and one without portfolio. Deputy Prime Ministers are usually elder statesmen, former Prime Ministers, for instance, or leaders of one or more of the main parties in the governmental coalition, other than that to which the Prime Minister belongs. Ministers of State are often without Portfolio but may be entrusted with some special function, such as constitutional reform, or relations with the Council of Europe. Ministers, whose number varies between 15 and 25, are in charge of the principal government departments. Secretaries of State, of whom there may be as many as 15 or as few as 5, are junior ministers, to all intents and purposes equivalent to a British Under-Secretary of State. They may, however, be in charge of a subordinate department, or of one or more sections of a ministry. There are usually one or two Secretaries of State attached to the Prime Minister's Office; the Ministry of National Defence will include Secretaries of State for War, Air and the Navy, and the Ministry of Finance a Secretary of State charged with responsibility for the budget or fiscal reform; there may be a Secretary of State to deal with certain aspects of education, such as technical education or fine arts.

The office of Secretary of State was unknown during the Third Republic and the title was first used under the Vichy administration. There were, however, Under-Secretaries of State during the Third Republic and in some of the governments of the Fourth, but there seems to be a tendency for this office to disappear. No Under-Secretaries were appointed from 1949 to 1956. Secretaries of State do not attend meetings of the *Conseil des Ministres* unless the affairs of their departments are under discussion. Ministers of State, of course, do attend.

The Prime Minister sometimes himself takes charge of a department, usually either that of Foreign Affairs or of Finance, whichever is the key ministry at the time.

It is not necessary in France for either the Prime Minister or his colleagues to be members of one of the houses of parliament, though in practice they nearly always are. But, in 1946, M. Blum headed an interim government for a month, although he was not then a member of either house, and when he first became Prime Minister, in 1936, he appointed three women Under-Secretaries, although, at that time, women neither had the vote nor were eligible for election to parliament. By virtue of their office, the Prime Minister, and also his colleagues, are entitled to attend meetings of either house and to speak, and also to attend meetings of the parliamentary Commissions. This provision, of course, renders unnecessary anything like the British requirement that a minimum number of ministers must be members of the upper house.

Co-ordination between Government Departments. The work of the different departments is co-ordinated by means of cabinet meetings, and inter-departmental meetings, and with the assistance of the Prime Minister's Office (*Secrétariat à la Présidence du Conseil*). Cabinet meetings are of two kinds. The *Conseil des Ministres* is a formal meeting of heads of departments, presided over by the President of the Republic. The *Conseil de Cabinet* is a meeting of members of the government, including Secretaries or Under-Secretaries of State, presided over by the Prime Minister. There are a number of smaller inter-departmental committees, either permanent, such as those concerned with defence or economic matters, or set up to deal with specific problems, such as the committees dealing with the Monnet Plan, or with European economic co-operation.

The Prime Minister's Office has two functions. As the cabinet secretariat it is responsible for the preparation of the agenda and the minutes of cabinet meetings;

it sees government bills through the different stages involved in their preparation, ensuring, for example, that all relevant ministries have been duly consulted and that the drafting has been approved by the Council of State; it includes a number of information services used by the Prime Minister and his colleagues; it approves the official text of ministerial orders, decrees and laws, for publication in the *Journal Officiel*; it is the recipient of written parliamentary questions submitted by deputies and is responsible for the distribution to them of the texts of bills.

The Prime Minister's Office also has attached to it a variable number of government departments, sometimes, though not always, under the control of a Secretary of State. These, by virtue of their direct responsibility to the Prime Minister, enjoy a greater degree of freedom from parliamentary interference than others. They have usually included the press, radio, and information services, the Commissariat for the Monnet Plan and the department concerned with the general co-ordination of the civil service.

The Structure of Government Departments. The structure of a French ministry differs in several ways from that of a British ministry. Perhaps the most striking difference is the existence in France of the *Cabinet*, a handful of personal assistants to the minister, appointed by and responsible to him. He is free to appoint anyone he likes, including friends or members of his family, since members of the *Cabinet* are not regular civil servants and their tenure of office is co-terminous with that of the minister. Or rather, they are not, in their capacity of members of a ministerial *Cabinet*, civil servants. They are often chosen from the body of permanent officials and are in that case seconded from their regular posts for as long as the minister needs them.

As the minister's private brains trust, members of the *Cabinet* combine the functions of a British minister's personal private secretary, with some of those of his Parliamentary Private Secretary[1] and of his permanent Under-Secretary, neither of the two last-mentioned offices having any equivalent in France. They prepare his speeches, answer his correspondence, help to ensure co-ordination between the minister and his civil servants and sometimes between the different departments within the ministry. At its best, the system helps to secure a better understanding between politicians and technicians. At its worst, it can be a form of nepotism.

A French ministry is divided into a variable number of *directions*, each representing one facet of the work of the department. Thus, the Ministry of Labour and Social Security has five *directions*, the Post Office six, and the Ministry of War twenty-two. The *directeurs* occupy the key posts in a Ministry. They have direct access to the minister or at least to his *Cabinet*, are responsible for briefing him and have, subject to his authority, complete control over their own departments. Their role in determining policy is important and, for this reason, their appointment is subject to special rules. *Directeurs* are nominated by (and can also be dismissed by) the *Conseil des Ministres* and may be chosen from outside the ranks of regular civil servants. In practice, they are generally high civil servants, sometimes detached from another service, the Council of State for instance, or they may be university teachers or administrators. As *directeurs* they do not enjoy security of tenure.

[1] Unlike the PPS, the members of the *Cabinet* are not, of course, members of parliament.

There is, as has been said, no equivalent in the French system of the British Permanent Under-Secretary. In some ministries there are officials called *secrétaires généraux*, but these titles are either survivals from some previous form of administration or else indications of some special function. Thus, for instance, one of the *directeurs* of the Post Office has the title of *secrètaire général* which has survived from the time when the Post Office was attached to the Prime Minister's Office. The *secrétaire général* of the government attends Cabinet meetings and is responsible for taking the minutes.

There are at least two explanations for the French ministry's lack of an administrative head, entrusted with the task of directing its general policy and co-ordinating the work of the different *directions*. The first is the traditional French suspicion of executive power, the insistence that acts of the executive must be closely supervised by the sovereign parliament. This fear is not, perhaps, without some foundation in a system in which ministers come and go as frequently as they do in France. A permanent official, who, as such, escapes the scrutiny of parliament, might, if he had the authority and prestige of a British Permanent Under-Secretary, become too powerful. The second explanation is that the office of Secretary-General was introduced under the Vichy régime and is therefore unpopular because of its association with that unhappy period.

Below the *direction*, there is considerable variety in the organization of the different ministries. There has been a tendency since the war for the internal structure of ministries to be modified in order to reduce the rigidity which has been one of the main characteristics of the French administration. There is, however, a certain general pattern. *Directions* are usually subdivided into a number of *Bureaux*, headed by *chefs* and *sous-chefs*. All these posts are filled from the ranks of the permanent civil service.

The Civil Service. In the French system, characterized as it is by governmental instability, the permanent officials play an essential role in maintaining the necessary continuity of administration. The French public service (*la fonction publique*) includes all state employees—teachers, local government officials, industrial and postal workers. It numbers nearly a million (excluding, of course, professional soldiers), of whom nine-tenths are employed by the Ministries of Education, Defence, Finance, Public Works, the Interior, and the Post Office. The government departments in Paris (*les Administrations Centrales*) are staffed by some 30,000 to 40,000 civil servants, grouped in 20 to 30 different ministries.

Up to the war, civil servants were divided into a complex and over-rigid hierarchy of grades. These differed from one ministry to another, as did the entrance examinations. Since the war, the status and working conditions of civil servants have been redefined by law and the different grades have been reorganized into four main categories, roughly equivalent to the British classification into administrative, executive, technical, and clerical grades. A special department attached to the Prime Minister's Office is responsible for ensuring co-ordination and unification. Its functions are much more restricted than those of the Establishment Branch of the Treasury, however. In France there is no single body entrusted with general responsibility for the running of the civil service. Each ministry retains responsibility for its own staff. But the *Direction de la Fonction*

Publique of the Prime Minister's Office sees that there is uniformity of salaries and conditions and determines the policy of the National School of Administration from which all higher civil servants are now recruited.

Candidates for the higher, or administrative, grade of the civil service usually enter the National School of Administration for a three-year course after they have completed a course of training, either at a university or at one of the seven *Instituts d'Etudes Politiques*, of which the best known is that in Paris, known before the war as the *Ecole des Sciences Politiques*. The basis of recruitment has been broadened since the war, in order to allow candidates who have not been able to follow this type of course to compete on equal terms with the others. Half the vacancies in the National School are reserved for candidates having already completed four years' service in an executive grade, for whom the entry qualifications are less severe. Once they have been admitted to the School, no discrimination is made between the two types of entrant.

It is hoped that the new methods of training will not merely attract candidates from a wider field, but will also end the compartmentalization from which the pre-war service suffered. The greater prestige of certain departments, known as *les grands Corps*—that is, the Council of State, the Court of Accounts, the Ministry of Foreign Affairs, and the *Inspection des Finances*—led in the past to too great a concentration of talent in these departments at the expense of the others, which candidates tended to rate as second best. While recruitment remained departmental, it was difficult to remedy this. Now, the unification of conditions of entry throughout the service and the reservation of a third of the posts in these coveted services to entrants from within the service should lead to a general raising of the standard in all departments. Methods of training, too, have been modified since the war. The somewhat arid intellectualism characteristic of the pre-war examination has given way to a training which places far more emphasis on practical experience of the working, not only of government departments, but also of private industry and commerce. The present aim is to mitigate the civil servant's isolation, to teach him to get to know people as individuals in society, before he becomes a bureaucrat who tends to regard them only as *administrés*. The final examination is now less rigidly specialized, though to British minds it remains primarily a test of intellectual, rather than of administrative qualities.

In France, the civil servant has a special legal status. This was defined by a law of 1946, the *Statut général des Fonctionnaires*, which replaces a number of earlier provisions governing different categories. It lays down general rules governing recruitment, conditions of employment, promotion, disciplinary processes and so on, classifies the different positions held by civil servants, defines guarantees of permanency and rights of appeal against actions by the official's superiors. It also recognizes the right of civil servants to belong to trade unions —a right which has frequently been challenged, even in the recent past.

Advisory and supervisory organs. Certain of the ministries, Defence, the Post Office, Public Works, Reconstruction, Health, and Education, for instance, have advisory committees (*Conseils Supérieurs*), generally composed, in part of high officials, in part of professional representatives, either appointed by the minister or elected by the interests concerned. Thus, the *Conseil*

8

Supérieur de l'Education Nationale has some seventy members, consisting of officials of the ministry, together with the representatives of the different branches of education. Its function is to advise the minister on a certain number of educational matters and to act as a Court of Appeal in disciplinary matters. Among these bodies, the greatest prestige attaches to the *Conseil Supérieur de la Défense Nationale* and the *Comité de Défense Nationale*, both of which are presided over by the President of the Republic. The *Conseil Supérieur de la Magistrature* is not an advisory body of this kind, but an executive organ.[1]

The work of the administration is subject to both financial and administrative supervision. Departmental supervision of the provincial branches of ministries (*les services extérieurs*) is carried out by an inspectorate which constitutes a department of the ministry in Paris. Thus, the *Inspection générale de l'Administration* of the Ministry of the Interior supervises the personnel of establishments coming under the Ministry of the Interior, such as prefectures, prisons, and police services; the *Inspection générale de l'Education Nationale* is responsible for the regular inspection of all schools; the *Inspection générale des Finances* supervises all *services extérieurs* of the Ministry of Finance. The *Inspection générale des Finances* also exercises financial supervision over a number of other bodies, including the Post Office, the railways, savings banks and the social security services. Its officials have great prestige and its members, like those of the Council of State, are frequently seconded for special service, either in ministerial *Cabinets* or in other departments of the administration. It should be added, however, that the Ministry of Finance does not enjoy

[1] *v.* below, p. 120.

the pre-eminence among government departments enjoyed by the British Treasury. It has not the authority to revise estimates, nor does it control the civil service. In theory it is a ministry like any other, though the nature of its functions naturally gives it a wider sphere of influence.

General financial control belongs to the Court of Accounts (*Cour des Comptes*), an independent body, whose members are appointed, like judges, for life and are irremovable. The constitution (article 18) entrusts to this body the task of assisting the National Assembly in supervising public accounts. It audits the accounts of government departments and of the social security services and publishes an annual report in the *Journal Officiel*, in which it comments on the efficiency of selected services as well as on their accounting. It also plays a large part in the work of two other organs of control. The first is the body set up in 1948 to inspect the accounts of the nationalized industries (*la Commission de Vérification des Comptes des Entreprises Publiques*); the second (*la Cour de Discipline Budgétaire*), set up in 1948, was empowered to impose penalties, which can amount to the loss of a year's salary, on civil servants found guilty of financial irregularities. Where the minister himself is held to be responsible, the court reports the matter to parliament.

The Council of State. The supreme organ of supervision of the administration is the Council of State (*Conseil d'Etat*). This body has, in reality, three distinct functions. First, it is the expert adviser of the government. It advises on the drafting of bills, decrees and ministerial orders, all of which must be submitted to it. It also advises government departments on administrative problems, on the interpretation of obscure or conflicting regulations, for instance, or on difficulties arising from inter-ministerial or inter-departmental disagreements, or from the application of certain administrative provisions laid down by its own judicial section. It may, also, take the initiative in proposing administrative reforms to the appropriate departments, or to the government. Up to 1958, it had only once used its other new right, namely, to suggest legislation.

Secondly, as an organ of administrative control (*tutelle administrative*) the Council plays a large part in the supervision of the work of local authorities.[1] It has also been entrusted with the task of inspecting and advising the local Assemblies set up since the war in the Overseas Territories,[2] and it also helps to supervise certain of the activities of quasi-independent bodies, such as the nationalized industries, authorizes the formation of religious orders or Friendly Societies and decides which associations are to have the right to acquire property or receive legacies.

To carry out its administrative functions, the Council of State is divided into four sections, called, respectively, the Sections for the Interior, for Finance, for Public Works and the Social Section. Each of these deals in reality with the business of a number of government departments, in addition to the one indicated by its name.[3]

[1] See Chapter VI, p. 138.
[2] See Chapter VII, p. 155.
[3] The four sections share out the work as follows:
    (i) The Interior, the Prime Minister's Office, the Offices of the Ministers of State, the Ministries of Education and Justice.
    (ii) The Departments of Finance, Foreign Affairs, Defence and Colonies.
    (iii) Departments dealing with economic affairs.
    (iv) Departments dealing with social affairs.

The third function of the Council of State is judicial. As an administrative body, it can only advise. The government is, in many cases, bound to consult it, but is, in theory, not bound to accept its advice, though, in practice, it usually does so automatically. As a judicial body, however, the Council of State gives decisions which have force of law. Indeed, refusal to carry out the decision of the Council of State constitutes an offence in itself and makes the offender liable to further penalties. These judicial functions are exercised by a fifth section (*Section du Contentieux*), which deals with disputes between different administrative services, and also with cases in which the citizen believes himself to have been wronged by the action of a state official, acting in his public capacity. It deals with such cases either directly, acting as a Court of First Instance, or indirectly as a Court of Appeal from local administrative courts (the former *Conseils de Préfecture*, which deal mainly with tax assessments) or other specialized tribunals, such as the *Conseil Supérieur de l'Education Nationale* or the *Cour des Comptes*, from whose judgments an appeal to the Council of State can be made on the grounds that they are *ultra vires*.

The existence of this supreme administrative court, alongside the ordinary civil courts, is due in the first place to the French adherence to the doctrine of the separation of powers. The idea that the civil servant is not subject in the same way as other citizens to the ordinary law of the land has, in the past, been criticized by British constitutional lawyers and, in particular, by Dicey.

'In France,' he said, 'officials are, or have been, in their official capacity, to some extent exempted from the ordinary law of the land, protected from the jurisdiction of the ordinary tribunals and subject in certain respects only to official law administered by official bodies.'[1]

This description certainly does not convey an accurate impression of the French system. Many lawyers now maintain that the criticism implied by Dicey, namely, that administrative law is liable to be biased in favour of the government, has long ceased to have any basis in fact. Administrative courts have built up a body of case law, which they use (though they are not bound by it) and they are fully as independent of the government as are the judges of the civil courts. Numerous cases can be cited of quite striking decisions against the government. To quote only one, in 1936, the socialist Minister of the Interior, M. Dormoy, removed from office a mayor of the Paris suburb of Saint-Denis, a deputy, M. Doriot, an ex-communist and the founder of a fascist organization, the French Popular Party. The Council of State, none of whose members was likely to have had much love for M. Doriot, rescinded the minister's decree. Nowadays, to quote an example such as this is in itself misleading, for, in the words of one barrister, practising both in the Council of State and the Supreme Court of Appeal (*la Cour de Cassation*),

'Councillors of State constitute the most respected and the most independent jurisdiction in France. Not a week passes without government acts being annulled and the state being sentenced to pay sums of money —often large sums—by these men who are liable to dismissal at the government's pleasure.'

Lawyers today defend the system on three main

[1] *The Law of the Constitution*, 8th edition, p. 190.

grounds. First, it permits, they say, a much more effective protection of the citizen against encroachments by the state than does, say, the British system, because governmental acts can be challenged not merely on the ground of *ultra vires*, but also on the ground of misuse of powers (*détournement de pouvoirs*). This extends the liability of officials to be called to account to include acts which may be technically legal, but are morally indefensible, because they were carried out with intentions contrary to those expressed by the legislator. Second, the citizen is more effectively compensated for any damage suffered by him, when damages are payable by the state. Indeed, it is frequently said that wherever any doubt exists regarding the private or public nature of the act in question, the bias is always in favour of making the state pay. Third, administrative procedure is both cheaper and speedier than that of the civil courts. The Council of State, says one authority,

'is the great protector of the rights of property and of the rights of the individual against the state; it is the great redresser of wrongs committed by the state'.[1]

With the vast extension in recent years of the scope of state intervention in the life of the ordinary citizen, and the consequent development of ministerial bodies with quasi-judicial powers, recognition of the real advantages possessed by the French system has become more general, and a number of European countries have created administrative courts, directly modelled on the French system.

The existence of two sets of courts does, however, create a technical difficulty. The official, of course,

[1] Barthélemy, J., *Le Gouvernement de la France* (Payot, 1939), p. 206.

remains personally responsible for acts committed in his private capacity and cases involving such acts are tried by the ordinary courts. In practice, it is not always easy to draw the line and it is possible for both courts to refuse jurisdiction. Where any doubt exists, the matter is referred to the *Tribunal des Conflits*, a body composed of representatives of both the Council of State and the *Cour de Cassation*, which decides whether jurisdiction belongs to the administrative or to the ordinary courts.

(b) ECONOMIC AND SOCIAL ADMINISTRATION

The nationalization of a number of basic industries in 1945 and 1946 and the setting up of the *Commissariat Général*, under the direction of M. Jean Monnet, to draw up a six-year plan for the reorganization and modernization of six of France's basic industries, inevitably led to the development of new forms of administration, with different organizations and methods from those of the civil service. French economic administration has been sometimes less and sometimes more subject to state control than British. For example, France has a national minimum wage, determined by the government on the advice of a Commission (*la Commission Supérieure des Conventions Collectives*), on which are represented the Ministry of Labour, the employers and the trade union confederations. In the interests of the national economy, post-war British governments maintained a whole series of controls over private producers, distributors and consumers, controls ranging from allocations of raw materials and the determination of export and import quotas to price control and consumer rationing. The post-war French state was never able to enforce respect for economic controls to anything like the same extent. On the other hand, the French system has always included a whole series of effective controls, imposed either by the state or by agreements between producers or distributors themselves, in the form of restrictive practices whose purpose is to further the interests of certain sections of the community, sometimes to the detriment of the interests of the community as a whole.

The nationalized industries. State control of certain sectors of the economy is no new thing in France. Apart from old *'manufactures royales'* such as those making Sèvres porcelain and Gobelins tapestries, traditional monopolies such as the tobacco, matches and playing card monopolies and such concerns as arsenals and the Post Office, France already had, before the war, a nationalized railway system, while the Bank of France and a number of armament industries were also state-controlled.

After the Second World War, the provisional governments nationalized the deposit banks, the mines, the gas and electricity industries, insurance, the merchant navy and civil aviation, in addition to assuming responsibility for the management of a number of concerns, of which the most important was the Renault motor works, whose owners had been guilty of collaboration with the enemy.

The administration of the nationalized industries presents a much tidier picture in France than does the heterogeneous collection of quasi-independent boards through which the British nationalized industries are administered. In general, France has rejected both the principle of direct administration by a government department, on the model of the Post Office, and that of quasi-independent administration by a body such as the National Coal Board. The general structure in France is tripartite, the governing body of the industry, and sometimes also of the undertakings themselves, includes representatives of the responsible government department, of the consuming interests and of the employees in the industry, the last-mentioned being represented by nominees of the different trade union confederations. In some cases there is also provision for the representation of technical experts. Power is divided between the director-general, the governing board, and the ministry, which usually has, in practice, the final say. The accounts of the nationalized industries are audited by the *Commission de Vérification des Comptes*, set up in 1948, and including representatives of the Ministries of Finance and Economic Affairs, which has wide powers of investigation and the right to make criticisms regarding the management in general. The Commission submits an annual report to the minister and to parliament. Some of the reports are published in the *Journal Officiel*.

There are considerable variations in the detailed structure of the different industries and, as far back as 1945, the Council of State suggested that the regulations should be unified. Though plans have been discussed, the idea has now been abandoned.

The Monnet Plan. The task of working out a general plan for the reorganization and modernization of French industry and agriculture was entrusted after the war to the *Commissariat Général du Plan de Modernisation et d'Equipement*, under the general direction of M. Jean Monnet. It included a number of technical committees, including representatives both of government departments and of the different branches of the economy, whose function was to draw up a comprehensive plan for the reorganization of six basic, or key, industries, those of coal, power, steel, building materials, agricultural machinery, and transport, together with plans for increases in production and productivity in other industries.

The long-term objectives and over-all requirements of capital and raw materials were translated into terms of annual credits or subsidies by the *Direction du Budget* of the Ministry of Finance. While acute shortages persisted, materials were allocated by the appropriate departments and the *Comité Inter-Ministériel Economique* supervised allocations, drew up export and import programmes and fixed prices of raw materials. Much of this apparatus of control was dropped as the economic system returned to its normal habits, and the necessary steps to carry out the Plan were taken by the relevant technical sections of the different ministries, the cabinet being responsible for decisions as between rival claimants and for the approval of the annual programme to be financed by the budget.

In the private sectors of industry, the carrying out of the Plan was provided for by agreements under which the major industries concerned undertook to take the necessary steps and the government to supply or to assist the industry to obtain the necessary finance or materials. In the case of smaller concerns, co-ordination was facilitated by the co-operation of regional advisory bodies, including, for example, members of chambers of commerce and trade union representatives.

In fact, French resources alone would have been totally inadequate to finance a plan on this scale and much of the necessary capital was supplied through Marshall Aid. The fifth (and final) annual report in 1953 announced the general completion of the first plan, with the exception of agriculture, where the achievement was considerably below expectations. The second plan was put into application in 1954, and a third had been prepared, and was ready to be placed before parliament by March 1958.

Social Security. The French social security services are administered very differently from those of Great Britain. The general picture is one of very great complexity, since older services still exist alongside the comprehensive service introduced in 1946, and because a number of industries—the mines, for example, the railways, agriculture and civil servants—have their own systems, which are administered separately from the general system.

It is necessary, too, to distinguish between services which are in the nature of assistance and those which can be described as social insurance. In the first category, there are family allowances, a special maternity allowance whose purpose is to encourage young couples to have children soon after marriage and at relatively frequent intervals, pre-natal and (since 1949) lodging allowances, and the allowance paid to families in which there is only one wage-earner. These are non-contributory, in the sense that no deduction is made from the workers' wages, but contributory in the sense that they are financed by payments made by employers, amounts being determined as a percentage of the wage bill. Benefits are not paid at flat rates but are calculated as percentages of a national 'basic wage' which is, in Paris, some 25 per cent below the level of the national minimum wage.

It has been calculated that, for a family in which there are three children and only the father works, they amount to about three-quarters of the national minimum wage. In 1958, a Paris family with two children, and only the father working, would receive over 12,000 francs a month.

There is no national unemployment insurance, assistance to unemployed workers remaining a local responsibility. Social insurance therefore covers a much narrower field than in Great Britain. It covers sickness, normal maternity benefits, industrial injury, old age, and death benefits. Hospital and dental treatment are provided, but doctors are left free to treat their patients and charge them in the normal way, a high percentage of the amounts then being recoverable by the insured person from his social security branch.

The service is administered, not by a government department, but by representatives elected by the insured persons themselves. Local and regional offices (the family allowances having their own separate administration) are governed by boards, elected as to almost three-quarters by representatives of the trade union confederations, each being allotted a definite proportion, and as to a quarter by representatives of the employers. The state's participation takes three forms. There is a national fund, which serves as an equalization fund, and there have been annual subsidies to make good the deficit which has hitherto been a regular feature. The state also supervises the accounts, which are audited by a committee of the Court of Accounts. This body also scrutinizes the management of the services and makes a report, including criticisms and recommendations, which is published in the *Journal Officiel*. Thirdly, the *Direction générale de la Sécurité Sociale* of the Ministry of Labour and Social Security maintains general supervision and co-ordination and employs a staff of supervisors to inspect the administration of the services throughout the country.

Apart from the state contributions just mentioned, the French system is financed by contributions from employers and workers. The employers alone finance the Family Allowances Fund by a payment of 16 per cent of their wage bill, and also the Industrial Accidents Fund, payments to which vary, but average some 3 per cent of the wage bill. The other services are financed by payments made by the employers amounting to 16 per cent of the wage bill, of which 6 per cent is borne by the workers and deducted from their wages. It is obvious that, in a period of price inflation, such a system must incur a deficit, unless it has large reserves, since its receipts are determined by the level of wages, while its expenditure is determined by the price level.

The system has been criticized in France on the ground that it is an important contributory factor in the high cost of production, the total burden of contributions being in the region of 30 to 35 per cent of the total wage bill. On the other hand, it has been pointed out, first, that since the post-war wage bill, including social security payments, does not represent a larger share of the national income than it did before the war, all that has happened is that the worker now receives a larger share of the family income in this form; and second, that in a country which obtains only about 30 per cent of its revenue from direct taxation, and in which there is, in addition a high degree of tax evasion, the taxpayer cannot easily be induced to take the burden off the shoulders of the employer, except in the way that he does at present, namely, by paying higher prices.[1]

Workers' control in industry. Both the administration of the nationalized industries and that of the social

[1] A law of 1 July 1956 instituted an Old Age Pension fund to be financed out of taxation (mainly on cars) to enable the State to guarantee a minimum pension of 240,000 frances per annum (in 1958).

security services reveal the extent of the survival of earlier syndicalist tendencies, as well as the suspicion of authority which still characterizes the attitude of the average citizen. He feels that the workers in an industry, or the beneficiaries of social security, ought themselves to have a say in how the industry or the service is run. This conception also underlies the post-war institution of works committees (*Comités d'Entreprise*), which are obligatory in France in all industrial establishments employing fifty or more workers. They are intended to associate the worker with the running of industry and, in the minds of some, to lead to his having an effective share in management. So far, their functions have remained advisory. They have the right, however, to manage welfare services and to see the firm's statement of accounts, including profits. In large concerns they are entitled to the assistance of a trained accountant to enable them to understand them. The committees also have representatives on the governing boards.

Different categories of personnel, including technicians and foremen, are elected as members of the committees by the appropriate professional organizations in proportion to their numbers in the establishment. The employer or his representative presides, but if he fails to carry out this duty, he is replaced by the Inspector of Labour (a ministry official) who is entitled to resolve a certain number of differences: for example, concerning dismissals or the appointment of the company's doctor. The Inspector also has the committee's minutes communicated to him.

Works committees exist in those nationalized industries which do not constitute state monopolies—in insurance, for example, or the Renault works. In those nationalized industries which have a special legal status, as for example the railways, the mines or the Paris Underground, special rules are laid down governing the constitution and functions of the committees.

(c) THE JUDICIAL FRAMEWORK

In both the Administrative and the ordinary courts, the administration of justice is based on two fundamental principles: the first is that, except for local courts, where minor offences are dealt with by the *Juge de paix*, judges in France do not sit alone; the second (again with the exception of minor offences punishable by a small fine) is that there is always a right of appeal.

The organization of the Courts. Civil Courts include those of the *Juge de paix*, which serve from two to five *cantons*, and the Civil Courts of First Instance which serve the *arrondissement* or several *arrondissements*. The *Juge de paix*, unlike the British Justice of the Peace, is a trained lawyer. His function is mainly to persuade contestants to agree to settlements out of court and to try minor cases, involving, for instance, such things as rights of way. He sits alone and is assisted by an official of the court (*greffier*). The Civil Court of First Instance is competent to try all civil cases and also to hear appeals from the *Juge de paix* and from the *Conseil de Prud'hommes*. It also deals, for example, with such matters as matrimonial cases. It is presided over by a judge, assisted by two assessors, who have an equal voice in deciding on the verdict.

Conseils de Prud'hommes deal with differences between workers and employers. They are organized on a functional basis, separate courts being constituted to deal respectively with industrial, agricultural and commercial matters, where there exists a need for them.

The *Conseil de Prud'hommes*, consisting half of employers and half of workers, is elected by and from members of these two categories, in the industry over which it has jurisdiction. Formalities and cost are reduced to a minimum and efforts are made to settle problems by agreement, where possible. In large centres, there is a *Tribunal de Commerce* which deals with commercial cases, including bankruptcies. There is an appeal from its verdicts to the Court of Appeal.

Criminal courts deal with three types of offence. Minor offences (*contraventions*) equivalent, say, to a summons for failure to have a bicycle lamp or a number plate, or for obstruction of the highway, are dealt with in the *Tribunal de Simple Police* by the *Juge de paix*, who imposes a fine or a period of imprisonment not exceeding a few days. More serious offences (*délits*), such as adulteration of milk, housebreaking or assault, are dealt with by the *Tribunal Correctionnel*. Here the procedure is much more formal and the prosecution is represented by prosecuting counsel, permanently employed by the Department of the Public Prosecutor. Courts of First Instance may be divided into Civil and Criminal (*Correctionnel*) sections, or the same court may sit in the two capacities on different days. Very serious crimes, such as arson and murder, are dealt with by the Courts of Assize, of which there is one in each *département*. They are tried before a jury of seven, by a presiding judge (who is a *Conseiller à la Cour d'Appel*) and two assistant judges. The jury's decision does not have to be unanimous in France; a majority suffices. The jury also has a voice in the determination of the sentence.

Appeals from cases dealt with in Courts of First Instance go to the regional Court of Appeal. There are twenty-seven Appeal Court regions, whose courts are divided into sections (*Chambres*) dealing with the different types of case. Appeal goes in the final instance, and directly in the case of offences dealt with by Assize Courts, to the Supreme Court of Appeal, the *Cour de Cassation*.

As its name implies, this court is competent to quash verdicts. It does not itself deliver a final verdict, as does the House of Lords, but merely decides whether the verdict from which there is an appeal was correct in law. If the decision is that it was not, the case is sent back for retrial by a court of the same type as that which first tried it. If this Court repeats the first verdict after a second trial, the conflict between the Court and the *Cour de Cassation* is resolved by a decision of the *Cour de Cassation* at a plenary session. The case is then referred to a third Court, which must concur.

The *Conseil Supérieur de la Magistrature*, created by the constitution of 1946, is the body responsible for administering the courts and, through its control of the appointment and promotion of judges, for ensuring the independence of the judiciary. It is presided over by the President of the Republic, and the Minister of Justice is its vice-president.[1] It also advises the President on the exercise of his right of pardon and commutation of sentences.

One or two striking differences from the British system should be noted. First, there are state advocates, permanently employed by the Ministry of Justice, who act for the prosecution in criminal cases. They are known as members of the *parquet*, as opposed to *avocats* who are

[1] The Council consists of twelve members in addition to its President and Vice-President. Two are nominated by the President, six by the National Assembly, from outside its own ranks, four by different categories of the legal profession. (Constitution, article 83.)

in private practice. The *parquet* is known as *la magistrature debout*, as opposed to judges, who constitute *la magistrature assise*.

French legal procedure, too, differs greatly from that of British courts. The accused is not brought immediately before a court, which decides whether there is a *prima facie* case. That function is entrusted to an examining magistrate (*juge d'instruction*). He examines the evidence, interrogates the prisoner and examines witnesses in private. The report of this examination is communicated to the *Chambre des mises en accusation*, which then decides, in the light of it, whether he is to be brought to trial. There is a jury only in the Assize Courts and its recommendations, as for instance the indication of extenuating circumstances when there has been a finding of guilt in a murder case, limit the judge's discretion in imposing sentence.

It can be argued in favour of this system that it prevents a number of cases from ever coming into court. To British minds, one strong objection to the French system would be the possibility which it affords to the authorities of keeping an accused person in custody for long periods, sometimes amounting to years, before any decision is taken to bring him to trial.

French legal theory insists that an accused person is not guilty until so proved. But the methods of establishing innocence or guilt are so different from those of Great Britain that they might at times appear to British observers to imply an assumption of guilt. The presiding judge does not, as in Great Britain, remain in the background, intervening only to hold the scales fairly between prosecution and defence. It is his function to lead the investigation which is to decide on the prisoner's innocence or guilt. He plays an active part in the interrogation, instead of leaving it largely to Counsel. The investigation itself is much more wide-ranging, taking into account personal background as well as the background of the facts in the case. This wider view-point probably explains in part why much evidence that would be ruled inadmissible in an English court is admissible in a French court.

In France, both civil and criminal law are codified. This has the advantage of giving greater precision and uniformity. It might be assumed that an accompanying disadvantage would be a loss of the elasticity and adaptability claimed for British case law. But many experts in comparative law now doubt whether, in fact, this is so.

CHAPTER VI

LOCAL GOVERNMENT

The French approach to Local Government. A British student of political science who tries on the eve of his final examination to acquire at least a hazy grasp of the outlines of French local government could be forgiven for concluding that no such thing exists. His university library will have upwards of a dozen up-to-date and detailed accounts of British local government. But it will contain only one study of French local government and that written by an Englishman.[1] If he consults French text-books, he will find that treatises on constitutional law, or on the French system of government, either do not mention local government at all, or else accord it a few pages only, as part of a section entitled 'Administration'. Local government is, indeed, usually treated either as part of administrative law, or else in hand-books for the use of mayors and municipal councillors, and the treatment of the subject is almost exclusively theoretical, dealing with electoral rules and the formal attributes of elected assemblies and their executive officers as laid down by different laws and decrees. The British student will glean from these no real picture of what a French local council actually

---

[1] Brian Chapman, *Introduction to French Local Government* (Allen and Unwin, 1953). This chapter owes much to Mr. Chapman's book, as also to the standard French works on administrative law.

does and of the part that it plays in the life of the community.[1]

One reason for this is that local authorities enjoy far less independence and initiative in France than they do in Great Britain. The framework of French local administration has remained substantially unchanged since Napoleon I introduced a tightly knit and highly centralized system in the year VIII. Up to the Revolution, France was divided, for administrative purposes, into a number of provinces, of very varied size and importance, and with strongly diversified regional characteristics. The revolutionaries did away with these traditional local areas and substituted for them *départements*, of much more nearly equal size, with different names from those of the former provinces and each with the same system of administration.[2] Napoleon subordinated the local assemblies in these *départements* to the control of a prefect, appointed by and responsible to the government in Paris. It was not until the Third Republic that democratically elected local assemblies became organs with real, though still limited, powers of self-government, or more accurately, of self-administration.

The pattern of local government. The democratic institution of the elected council was, however, grafted on to the Napoleonic framework, rather than substituted for it. For purposes of local government France's ninety[3]

---

[1] *L'administration régionale et locale de la France*, by Hervé Ditton (Presses Universitaires de France, 1953), does adopt a much more realistic approach.

[2] There has been considerable argument regarding the degree of artificiality of departmental boundaries, as compared with those of the old provinces, and the extent to which the Revolutionaries were endeavouring to kill provincial loyalties, or were trying, on the contrary, to base the new boundaries on geographical realities and local feeling.

[3] Including the Territoire de Belfort, but excluding the

départements are divided and subdivided into 311 *arrondissements* (of which there are on an average three to five per *département*), some 3,000 *cantons* (five or six per *arrondissement* and thirty-six per *département*) and some 38,000 *communes* (a *département* containing, on an average, between 400 and 500 *communes* and an *arrondissement* about a hundred so so).[1]

In each of these four categories, every area has the same system of administration, however great the disparities of size and population and however much their regional or economic characteristics differ. The only exceptions to this uniform pattern are the three large towns of Paris, Lyons and Marseilles, the *département* of the Seine and, in one important respect, the three *départements* of Alsace-Lorraine.

This does not mean, of course, that all towns, whatever their size, do exactly the same things. Towns are required to undertake different functions in accordance with the size of their population.[2] But all towns classed in one category—for instance as *communes* of under or over 10,000, or 20,000 inhabitants—have identical obligations which must be fulfilled in identical ways. The symmetrical French pattern makes no administrative distinction between urban and rural districts; there are no independent enclaves such as the British County Borough; there are no individual towns with special rights which others in the same category do not possess. There is no equivalent of the British private bill to give

twelve Algerian and four 'overseas' *départements*, on which *v.* Chapter VII.

[1] The Nord, with two million inhabitants and highly industrialized, has 6 *arrondissements*, 68 *cantons* and 669 *communes*. Pyrenées Orientales, a rural *département* with 228,000 inhabitants, has three *arrondissements*, 18 *cantons* and 233 *communes*.

[2] There are also, of course, optional powers which some *départements* take advantage of.

special rights to particular authorities. Status determines function.

In practice, the only two local government units that matter are the *département* and the *commune*. The *arrondissement* and the *canton* are today merely administrative conveniences, though both are local centres for a number of government departments. The *arrondissement* is administered by a sub-prefect, to whom the prefect delegates some of his responsibilities, particularly in regard to the supervision of the smaller *communes*. The *canton* is the constituency for the Departmental Council elections.

The average size of a *département* is about 2,000 square miles, with a population of about half a million—that is, about the size and population of Norfolk. The largest (Gironde) is almost twice as large, and the smallest (Rhône) only just over half as large.[1] The most sparsely populated (Basses Alpes) has 83,000 inhabitants and covers an area slightly smaller than that of Devonshire, whose administrative county includes a population of half a million. The most populous (Nord) has almost two million inhabitants.

Departmental Councils. The Council for the *département* is elected normally in October, each *canton*, irrespective of size,[2] electing one councillor for six years. One half of the councillors retire every three years, the two 'series' of *cantons* being constituted

[1] This statement leaves out of account the Territoire de Belfort and the *département* of the Seine.

[2] Since the boundaries of *cantons* are still in the main the same as they were in the nineteenth century, their population varies widely. Thus, for example, the *canton* of Coursegoules (Alpes Maritimes), which has 893·inhabitants, elects one councillor, as does the *canton* of Nice with 102,617 inhabitants. The *département* has in all 449,000 inhabitants in thirty cantons, and so elects thirty councillors.

arbitrarily and not on any geographical basis. The Councils were reconstituted in 1945; subsequent elections took place in March 1949 and in October 1951. Men and women are entitled to vote if their names are on the national electoral register. Candidates must be not less than twenty-three years of age. A first ballot is held, at which all candidates receiving an absolute majority of the votes cast (that is, a half plus one) are declared elected; a week later (that is, the following Sunday), a second ballot is held where necessary. At this, only a relative majority is required.

The average membership of Councils is thirty-six, though the rural *département* of Pyrenées Orientales has only eighteen and the heavily industrialized *département* of the Nord has sixty-eight. They meet in two ordinary sessions, the first in April–May, lasting not more than a fortnight, the second between August and October, lasting not more than a month. Special sessions may be called in one of four ways: by the President of the Republic; by the prefect; at the request of two-thirds of the members of the Council, or by the Departmental Commission of from four to seven councillors, elected in August by the Council, as a standing committee meeting once a month when the Council is not sitting.

Departmental Councils have five main functions. First, they are responsible for the upkeep of roads classed as departmental and of public buildings, whether these house state-controlled or departmental services. These include prefectures and sub-prefectures, schools and training colleges, assize courts, prisons, and so on. Secondly, they control the running of departmental services, such as public assistance, certain health services, public works, drainage, etc. Thirdly, they vote the annual budget. Local revenue is made up, on the one hand of receipts from certain local taxes—on public entertainments or the sale of spirits, and from licences—on dogs, billiard-tables, and so on, and on the other hand, of direct taxes, called 'additional centimes'.[1]

There are also state loans and subsidies, granted for approved departmental expenditure, mainly on public assistance. The financial powers of Councils are restricted and the budget is subject to the general approval of the Ministry of the Interior. Fourthly, Departmental Councils have some responsibility in certain matters concerning municipalities, such as the fixing of maximum rates for certain types of tax, the fixing of electoral boundaries, the classification of roads, the authorization of sites of markets or fair-grounds. Fifthly, they advise the Minister of the Interior when consulted, and are entitled to make recommendations on all matters relating to local administration, though not to pass resolutions on political (as distinct from administrative) matters.

Municipal Councils. Communes have councils of from 11 to 37 members according to the size of their population. Representation is not proportional to population, however, but is heavily overweighted in favour of small villages. The smallest have 11 members, and over half of them (22,665) have populations of less than 500.[2]

[1] These taxes are called 'additional centimes' because the amount to be levied is expressed as a percentage of the revenue from certain national taxes. But these taxes have not been levied since 1917. The system of assessment is, therefore, exceedingly complex, being based on a notional figure representing the revenue that would have been collected if the taxes were still being levied. For a full description of local finance, including 'additional centimes', v. Chapman, op. cit., Chapter 6.

[2] Five hundred and eighty-one have populations of under fifty.

Outside Paris, only 45 have over 60,000 inhabitants, entitling them to 37 members. Thus towns such as Besançon or Tours, with less than 100,000 inhabitants, have Councils numbering 37, as do towns such as Bordeaux and Nice, with populations of about a quarter of a million. Of the total of 466,209 councillors, over 450,000 represent communities with under 9,000 inhabitants and with a total population of 24 millions. The remaining 16 millions elect fewer than 13,000 councillors. This under-representation of large towns does not necessarily affect municipal administration seriously, but it does, of course, have repercussions on national representation, owing to the preponderance of municipal delegates in the electoral college which elects councillors of the Republic.[1]

Municipal councillors (who must be not less than twenty-three years of age) are elected in April or May, for six years, all retiring together.[2] In towns of over 9,000 inhabitants (of which there were 456 in 1953) election is by proportional representation. Each party seeking representation presents a list containing as many names as there are seats to be filled (from twenty-seven to thirty-seven), and obtains as many seats as its votes equal multiples of the quotient (the number of votes cast, divided by the number of seats). Voting is for individuals, not for the list as a whole, and voters can express a personal preference for a candidate or candidates and even cross a name out and substitute one from another party's list (the process known as *panachage*).

In *communes* with fewer than 9,000 inhabitants, election is by the double-ballot system, which has been the

[1] See Chapter III, p. 38.
[2] By-elections are not normally held to fill casual vacancies. Municipal elections were held in October 1947, and in the Spring of 1953.

rule since 1884. An absolute majority of the votes cast (a half plus one) is necessary to secure election at the first ballot; at the second a relative majority suffices. Again, each party list includes as many names as there are seats to be filled and the elector is free to express his personal preferences.[1]

Like the Departmental Council, the Municipal Council does not meet regularly throughout the year, but has four sessions, each lasting in principle about a fortnight, in February, May, August, and November. It can be specially convened if necessary, by either the mayor, the prefect or the sub-prefect, or at the request of one-third of the councillors. Its budgetary session may also be extended, if necessary, to six weeks, with the agreement of the sub-prefect.

The mayor is chosen for the full period of six years, by his fellow councillors, who also choose a number of deputy-mayors (*adjoints*)—from one to twelve according to the size of the *commune*.[2] Both mayors and deputy-mayors are usually party men, whereas British mayors are little, if anything, more than impartial chairmen during their period of office.

The *commune* is responsible for the upkeep of municipal roads and property, for decisions regarding the carrying out of public works, the wages of municipal employees, the organization of municipal services, such as the fire service, burials, slaughter-houses, public baths, etc. It votes the annual budget, which is drawn up by

[1] In principle, the whole *commune* forms a single constituency, but in cases where the village includes more than one agglomeration, it is possible for it to be divided into wards, in order to prevent any hamlet or district from being without a representative. The law of 1947, which governs the conduct of elections in towns of 9,000 or over, expressly excludes this possibility.

[2] Paris, Lyons and Marseilles have larger numbers.

the mayor, and it makes recommendations regarding the functioning of local services. Political recommendations are prohibited.

The restricted scope of local government authorities. To the British citizen, used to busy Borough and County Councils, meeting all the year round and, in the larger urban agglomerations, holding frequent committee meetings as well, it is evident that French local authorities, meeting as they do for only a few weeks in the year, cannot have a similar range of activities. In fact, not only do French local Councils deal with fewer matters than are dealt with by British local authorities, but they also play a far less direct and responsible role in the running of local affairs.

To begin with, a number of functions which, in Britain, are the concern of local authorities are, in France, the direct responsibility of the state, although councillors sometimes serve on the state organs in the *département*. Education, for example, is a state service, controlled by officials of the ministry. Teachers are not local government employees, but civil servants.[1] In towns with over 10,000 inhabitants, the police force is controlled (and largely paid for) by the state. In the rural areas, police duties are carried out by the *gendarmerie*, a military organization directly responsible to the Ministry of War. The British citizen pays his rates to the local authority at the Town Hall or Council offices. The

[1] Elementary teachers are appointed by the prefect, but on the recommendation of the *inspecteur d'académie*, an official of the Ministry of Education. Elementary education is organized by him, in conjunction with the prefect and a Departmental Education Council on which the Departmental Council is represented along with school inspectors nominated by the Ministry. There is no direct activity of the Council as such and no equivalent of the British local Education Committee.

Frenchman pays his local taxes to a tax-collector who is an official of the Ministry of Finance. A number of services are thus not 'local' at all in the British sense, but more nearly akin to local branches of the Ministry of National Insurance or the Post Office, the officials at the head of the local organization being civil servants directly appointed by the minister and responsible to him. The Departmental Council has no responsibility in the matter (except to provide the money for the upkeep of buildings).

The chief difference between French and British local government, however, lies in the French separation of executive from deliberative functions. In Great Britain, local services are run by the Council through its different committees, at which a permanent official of the local authority receives his instructions, later ratified by a full meeting of the Council. In France, even those services which are a local responsibility and the concern of the Departmental Council—such as unemployment relief and public assistance, social services, highways, certain health services—are not administered directly by it, but by the prefect acting on its behalf. Similarly, in the *communes*, it is not the Council itself, but the mayor, who is responsible for the carrying out of the Council's policy. The Council's function is to debate or to decide. The prefect and the mayor act, and the whole system of local administration hinges on the part played by these two officials.

The Prefect. The prefect is often described as the pivot of French administration. It has been claimed that he has 5,000 distinct functions and they are certainly so many and varied that a brief summary such as this cannot pretend to give a comprehensive description of what he does. Fortunately, it is simpler to describe what he *is*, and the importance of his role in local administration. He is essentially two things, first the state's chief representative in the *département* and, second, the agent of the Departmental Council.

An official, in effect appointed by and responsible to the Minister of the Interior, the prefect has judicial and political, as well as administrative duties. He can, for example, detain persons considered to be dangerous to the security of the state. One of his most important political duties is to keep the minister informed of the state of opinion in the *département*—a function which has often been regarded with suspicion as giving a very real pull at elections to the party whose nominee holds the portfolio of the Interior.

His administrative duties are threefold. First, he is responsible for the general maintenance of law and order in the *département* and can, in emergencies, exercise considerable powers on his own initiative. He also sees that legislation and government orders are properly applied and can, himself, issue a number of orders. Secondly, he is responsible for co-ordination between the different state-controlled services which have officers in the *département*. This task is a delicate one, because these officials are also subject to the direct authority of their respective ministries in Paris. Some state services are organized on a regional as well as a departmental basis, with different towns as their regional and departmental headquarters and differing regional boundaries. There are sixteen educational and nine military regions and twenty-seven Appeal Court regions. A populous *département* will have upwards of fifty or sixty services dependent on a dozen or so ministries. The single authority through whom all in the *département* must work is the prefect. They carry out the orders of their respective ministries under his authority and submit for his sanction their own suggestions for action.

The prefect's third administrative function is to exercise on behalf of the state a guiding and controlling influence in the local administration. He is the main instrument of the 'administrative tutelage' which is a characteristic feature of French local government. In relation to the Departmental Council, he acts rather as a watchdog, ensuring that its activities are properly carried out within the legal framework and, if necessary, calling the attention of the government to irregularities. It is, in general, for the government to take the necessary action. His powers over mayors and Municipal Councils are much more extensive. He can, for example, suspend for a time both a mayor and a Municipal Council or dismiss a municipal councillor.[1] He can step in and take over the responsibility for carrying out duties that the mayor has failed to perform satisfactorily. He can annul irregular decisions of the Municipal Council and a number of its valid decisions require his ratification to become effective. His approval is required for the municipal budget and his authorization for legitimate expenditure.

Since the prefect's other role is that of executive officer of the Departmental Council, he is at one and the same time its servant and, if not its master, its supervisor. As the agent of the *département*, it is his duty to determine and prepare the Council's agenda and to draw up the budget. He has the right to be present and to speak at Council meetings (though not to take the chair and not when his accounts are under discussion). He

---

[1] According to Mr. Chapman, some 300 Councils are dissolved every year, often merely for lack of a quorum (op. cit., p. 127). This is a small proportion of France's 38,000 *communes*.

is responsible for carrying out the Council's decisions and for engaging and supervising the necessary staff. Councils can, of course, and sometimes do assert themselves against the prefect, for example by refusing to vote funds. If the deadlock becomes prolonged, it has to be settled by the Minister of the Interior. In practice, relations are normally good.

The fact that the prefect is often accorded discretionary power to apply specific provisions of laws and decrees in the light of local needs, and that he also has the right to issue a number of orders on his own initiative, gives him a degree of discretion that can result in considerable differences as between one *département* and another. This, together with the existence of permissive powers of local authorities, contributes to make the picture of French local government much less uniform than a purely theoretical description of formal attributes would imply.

The sub-prefects are also public servants appointed by the government and now have delegated to them a number of the prefect's tutelage powers over the smaller *communes*. Since 1950, the prefect may also delegate some of his functions as executive officer to the sub-prefect, who acts also as advisor to the mayors within his jurisdiction.

The Mayor. Within his own smaller system, the mayor exercises functions analogous to those of the prefect. He, too, has a dual role, first as the representative of the state in the *commune*, in which capacity he is responsible to the prefect who is his hierarchical superior, and secondly, as the executive officer of the *département*, responsible to the Municipal Council, but subject to the 'administrative tutelage' of the prefect. As the chief elected officer of the *commune*, he presides over

10

Council meetings (except when his accounts are being passed).

As a representative of the state, the mayor is the official responsible for the application of government decrees and Acts of Parliament, for the maintenance of law and order,[1] the keeping of registers of births, deaths, marriages, land and electoral registers, and for the conduct of elections. He also officiates at the civil ceremony of marriage, which is the only one recognized by the state.

The personality of the mayor and the way in which he uses his powers on behalf of the area he administers can lead to important differences in the character and scope of the functions undertaken by different municipalities and the degree of success that they achieve. In general, it is not unfair to say that an energetic mayor, prepared to make full use of whatever opportunities there are for local initiative, can very considerably mitigate the repressive and apathy-forming effects of the system of administrative tutelage. This is not to deny that, compared with the freer British system, he is called upon to do it the hard way.

Paris and the département *of the Seine.* Paris and the eighty suburban *communes* that go to make up the *département* of the Seine present an exception to the general pattern of French local government. The *département* of the Seine has two prefects, the prefect of police and the prefect of the Seine, who act both as mayors and prefects, the first being responsible for all police functions,[2] the second for the normal administrative

---

[1] Since 1941, in towns of 10,000 inhabitants and over, the police are state-controlled and are under the supervision, not of the mayor, but of the prefect.

[2] The Paris prefect controls the Paris region, which includes parts of Seine-et-Marne and Seine-et-Oise, as well as the *département* of the Seine.

functions of mayors and prefects. The Departmental Council consists of 150 councillors, ninety being the members of the Municipal Council and the remaining sixty councillors representing the suburban *communes*. Elections are by proportional representation in special constituencies. The sixty councillors are re-elected every six years, as is the Municipal Council.

Both the Municipal and the Departmental Councils have more restricted powers than those of provincial Councils. Fewer matters are within their competence; prior authorization is required for more of their decisions; and the tutelage powers of the prefects and the minister are greater. The *département* of the Seine has no Departmental Commission. Both Councils have an elected President, but the two prefects are entitled to attend meetings and to speak.[1]

The right of appeal. The fact that French local authorities are subjected to so comprehensive a system of administrative tutelage implies, in a democracy, the existence of some right of appeal. A mayor whose orders are cancelled, or a Council whose decisions are challenged by a sub-prefect or by a prefect, can normally appeal from the sub-prefect to the prefect, or from the prefect to the minister. A Departmental Council can appeal directly to the minister if it finds itself at loggerheads with its prefect. And the minister is himself in some cases bound, and in general accustomed, to seek approval for his actions from the body which, as has been

---

[1] Paris, Lyons and Marseilles are divided for administrative purposes into *arrondissements*, each of which has its own mayor. The twenty Paris *arrondissements* each have a mayor nominated by the Government. The fourteen Lyons and nine Marseilles *arrondissements* have deputy-mayors elected by the Council and allocated to the *arrondissements* by the mayor. The heads of *arrondissements* carry out only those duties which mayors perform as agents of the state.

seen, is the supreme organ of unification, supervision and control of administrative activity, the Council of State.

The administrative and judicial role of the Council of State. The hierarchical supervision of local authorities, exercised by the prefect and the Ministry of the Interior, is thus supplemented by the supervision and, if necessary, the judicial control of the Council of State, whose *Section de l'Intérieur* is most closely concerned with local administration and remains in permanent contact with officials of the Ministry of the Interior. The Council of State may be called on to advise on the legality of administrative acts, as, for instance, on the right of a prefect to get rid of a mayor before his successor has been installed, or to determine the respective rights of *communes* and *départements* in the matter of the provision of sports stadia, or on the circumstances in which a local authority is entitled to terminate contracts, or on the rent which may be charged for a presbytery let to a church. . . . On many such questions, the relevant legislation or decrees give rise to problems of interpretation which it is the task of the Council of State to sort out and resolve.

Another of its functions at times is to advise the minister or his agents as to whether the activities of a local authority are or are not legal. Thus, in 1949, a grant by a Departmental Council to miners' families who were suffering on account of a strike, and the decision by another to support the World Peace Congress, were both held by the Council of State to be invalid, on the ground that the decisions were political, not administrative, and so were not within the competence of local councils. A number of difficulties arose over the application of the so-called Poinso-Chapuis decree of 1948.

This decree authorized assistance to needy families in order to help them to educate their children in private (that is, catholic) schools. Some Councils endeavoured to provide compensatory assistance for state schools, in forms which were not permitted by the terms of the decree.

The Council of State is also called on to pronounce on the advisability, as distinct from the legality, of certain projects of local authorities, such as, for instance, alterations of local boundaries, but French authorities have themselves found it difficult to define the precise limits of its right to intervene in this field.

The government hardly ever fails to follow the Council's advice, especially when the issue is one of legality. In reaching its decisions, the Council endeavours to apply general principles laid down by its judicial section in cases which have come before that section. For both citizens and local authorities are free to seek redress in administrative courts for alleged wrongful acts committed by authorities. On the local plane, the twenty-two Prefectoral Councils, each consisting of three or four councillors nominated by the government, advise the prefect, authorize certain legal proceedings and themselves adjudicate in some cases, in income-tax litigation, for instance, in disputes arising between Councils and contractors, or between *communes* and *départements*, in cases of disputed elections, and in actions for damages arising out of public works carried out by the local authority.

Appeals from decisions of the Prefectoral Council go to the Council of State, which can annul decisions of local authorities on grounds of *ultra vires*, award damages in cases of negligence and pronounce on the improper use of police power.

The system in practice. There have been a number of criticisms of the French local government system. One is that the *département* is too small to be an efficient administrative unit. A number of state services are organized regionally, but the state has only gradually and grudgingly permitted local authorities to co-operate in order to provide joint services. Since the thirties, however, *communes* and *départements* have had limited powers to do so. The Vichy government introduced during the war a regional organization and regional prefects, but this innovation did not survive. In 1948, after the strikes of the previous year, regional officials, known as *Igames* or super-prefects,[1] were appointed, with power to organize security measures in cases of emergency, but there has been no further move towards regionalism since the war.

It is perhaps in part because the French system gives so little scope for local initiative that a century and three-quarters after their official disappearance from the map, the old provinces still have for most Frenchmen as real an existence as the *département*—certainly as ethnic, cultural and gastronomic, if not political, entities. Every Frenchman thought of Laval as an Auvergnat not as a native of Puy-de-Dôme; Poincaré was a Lorrain, as is M. Robert Schuman. Normans have a reputation for hardheadedness, Bretons and Alsatians are thought of as ardent catholics, who have at times had tendencies towards separatism. The *commune* is a living entity, from the smallest village to the large town. Like the *département*, the *commune* enjoys only limited freedom of action, but it is, nevertheless, a traditional local area, with a

---

[1] Their official title is *Inspecteurs Généraux de l'Administration en Mission Extraordinaire*. There are eight of them, each operating in principle in a military region.

continuous history; and its executive officer, the mayor, however subject to prefectoral supervision, is, unlike the prefect, a local man, elected by his fellow councillors to represent the community. It is significant that one of the changes that the Fourth Republic hoped to introduce was to increase the prestige and power of the President of the Departmental Council and to diminish the power of the prefect.

The two chief obstacles to responsible local government are the centralizing tendencies of the government departments and the system of administrative tutelage. The officials of the different ministries naturally tend to look to Paris and the government departments have sometimes encouraged them to by-pass the prefect. It is true that the prefect also represents the state, but, in his capacity of representative of the *département*, he opposes increases of power to other government departments. There has been a tendency, too, for permission to local authorities to provide municipally owned or controlled services to be granted only grudgingly and then to be hedged round with restrictive conditions. This is a criticism addressed in the main to the Council of State, which is the body ultimately responsible for sanctioning local initiatives of this kind. Even where permissive decrees are not themselves restrictive, pressure is often brought to bear on authorities to conform to a model plan.

Criticism of administrative tutelage has been widespread for many years. At the end of the First World War, M. Herriot, Mayor of Lyons from 1905, wrote:

'The French *commune* . . . can act, develop and prosper, only by permission of irresponsible officialdom; reforms or innovations require the authorization of far-away scribes accustomed to interminable delays. It almost requires exorcism to "dig out" a local matter from a ministry (and particularly from our glorious Finance Ministry). . . . Even in war-time there has to be a decree issued by the President of the Republic before a big town can buy cast-iron pipes and sluice-valves—essential requirements for its piped-water system. . . . A mayor who wants to build municipal wash-houses or baths is dissuaded, on the ground that he is going in for municipal trading. Our whole system of administrative tutelage leads to paralysis or to suspicion of initiative.'[1]

After the Second World War, M. André Philip wrote:

'France has inherited from Napoleon a centralized administration which becomes, with every day that passes, a more cumbrous machine, a more red-tape-ridden bureaucracy. . . . When one has been in England and seen how self-government works in British cities, one sees all the more clearly what a crushing burden administrative tutelage is in our towns.'[2]

The reasons for its survival. Why then has so little been done to change the system?

There is no simple answer to this question. To say, as some Frenchmen have said that, once they reach government benches, the most ardent partisans of reform become converted to the system, because 'they hope, with the help of the prefect, to secure the victory of their party at the next elections',[3] is to take too cynical a view. To say that when, after the war, minds were ripe for

[1] Quoted in Ferrat, *La République à refaire* (Gallimard, 1945), p. 24.
[2] Ibid., p. 10.   [3] Ibid., p. 27.

change, circumstances were unpropitious, is at most only a partial explanation.[1] Certainly, a rigid and uniform system like the French is much more difficult to change than is the relatively decentralized, untidy British system. The French system is to some extent self-perpetuating, because the kinds of initiative and experiment which prepare people's minds for fruitful change are largely ruled out.

There are explanations, however, that go deeper than any of these. The fact that administrative tutelage involves delay and a frustrating amount of red tape has encouraged French citizens to look for short-cuts. And these have created links between national and local politics which are likely to prove difficult to break. Pressure by the deputy has sometimes proved a more effective spur to ministerial action in local matters than reiterated appeals from the local authority. And, since relatively little time is taken up by Council meetings, it is quite possible to combine the functions of councillor (or mayor) with that of deputy, or senator. About a third of French members of parliament are members of a Departmental Council, about one-third of the senators and a quarter of the deputies are mayors. The combination is doubly useful to those concerned, because local prominence is a valuable electoral asset! But it can create additional obstacles to stable parliamentary government, because conflict between local interests and party programmes increases the tendency of deputies to

[1] The parties most in favour of reform after the war, and mainly responsible for the constitution which promised reform, were also those which favoured state control in the economic field. Their centralizing and decentralizing tendencies were, therefore, to some extent, in conflict. It is also true that, in the disorganization of the immediate post-war period, the prefect was an indispensible instrument of government.

indiscipline and so makes governmental majorities even more precarious.

As organized at present, local Councils are not equipped to take on extensive administrative duties. A number of deputies and senators who are now combining local with national politics would perhaps not welcome having to choose between them. Moreover, even with their present restricted opportunities, communist-dominated Municipal Councils have considerably complicated the problem of local administration, and governments are not anxious to increase difficulties for themselves.

All of these reasons perhaps help to explain why the promise of an extension of departmental and municipal liberty held out in the new constitution have not so far been fulfilled.[1]

[1] Constitution of 27.10.46, articles 87, 89 and 105. Bills were introduced, in both 1943 and 1948, to implement the promises made in these articles, but they have so far not been translated into law.

CHAPTER VII

THE FRENCH UNION

The background. The history of the French colonial Empire falls into three main phases. The first, lasting up to the Revolution, was dominated by the mercantilist principles of Colbert and ended in the loss of all the overseas possessions, with the exception of the five Indian towns, St. Pierre-et-Miquelon, Guyana, the four *comptoirs* of Sénégal, Réunion, Martinique and Guadeloupe.

From the middle of the nineteenth century onwards, up to the outbreak of the Second World War, France built up a colonial empire second only to that of Great Britain.

In the 1830's and 1840's there were settlements in Oceania and French authority in Algeria was gradually strengthened, although conditions there remained unsettled throughout the Second Empire. In the 1860's there was expansion in parts of West Africa, Madagascar and Indo-China. But it was not until the 1880's that the real period of colonial expansion began. Tunisia became a Protectorate in 1884; Annam and Tonkin a few years later and the Union of Indo-China was formed in 1887. In 1889, the five West African colonies were grouped in a federation with Dakar as its capital. In 1910, the Equatorial African Federation was formed, with Brazzaville as its capital. Finally, in 1912, the Treaty of Fez made Morocco a Protectorate.

From the end of the nineteenth century, France began to build up the modern system of colonial administration by trained officials, directly responsible to Paris. A school for the training of colonial administrators was established in 1889. In 1894, a Ministry of Colonies was created to take over general responsibility for colonial administration. This was the period of the great French Empire builders, of Brazza in the Congo, of Gallieni in West Africa and Madagascar, of Lyautey in Morocco. On the eve of the First World War, the French Empire included a population of 48 millions, of whom about one and a quarter million were French settlers, most of them in North Africa. After the end of the First World War, the administration of the mandated territories of Togoland and the Cameroons, formerly part of the German colonial Empire, was entrusted to France, as was responsibility for the A mandates of Syria and Lebanon. By 1939, the Empire covered 12 million square kilometres (over four and three-quarter million square miles) and included more than 68 million people.

French colonial policy. French colonialism exhibited two contradictory tendencies. The traditional policy inherited from the Revolution was assimilative, deliberately encouraging the development of institutions binding the colonies more closely to the mother country. In particular, a number of the colonies were directly represented in the French parliament. Altogether, 20 of the 618 deputies in the pre-war French Chamber of Deputies, and 7 of the 320 senators represented colonies. Not all the colonies were represented, however, and in all but the 'old colonies' of Guadeloupe, Martinique, Guyana and Réunion (together with Sénégal) the franchise was restricted to the local French settlers, together with a handful of natives who had been granted

French citizenship. Of the colonial population of 68 million, two and a half million were French citizens or Europeans, and of these something under half a million were electors. Algeria, with a population of over 7 million had an electorate numbering about a quarter of a million; the five Indian Settlements, with a population of almost 300,000 had an electorate of 57,000; Cochin-China, with a population of four and a half million had an electorate of under 5,000.

It is easy to criticize colonial representation in the mother parliament as being largely a meaningless façade, since the bulk of legislation is concerned with the affairs of France, and since a handful of natives could not have any significant influence on decisions of the French parliament. It is nevertheless a fact that its existence was valued highly by the natives themselves, as was the extension to natives of French citizenship on which the right to vote depended. It did also help to create a climate in which race consciousness, and therefore a sense of race superiority, or race inferiority, played a much smaller role than in the British colonial system at that time. For example, in 1935 a coloured deputy (M. Candace from Sénégal) was Vice-President of the Chamber and the post-war Council of the Republic has been presided over by a coloured senator since March 1947.

For those who believed in the policy of assimilation, progress was conceived of in terms of the extension of such representation and of the evolution of internal administration along French lines, rather than in terms of the development of colonial government along lines determined, in part, by the history and habits of the colony. From the end of the nineteenth century onwards, however, the contrary tendency of 'association' came to predominate, largely under the influence of great colonial administrators such as Gallieni and Lyautey. The socialist party, which was in opposition, with the exception of the brief Popular Front interlude of 1936–7, remained on the whole faithful to the assimilative principle, in part because of doubts regarding the genuineness of the 'association' advocated by French governments and French colonial Governors. It was certainly never intended either to be, or to lead to, 'self-government' as the British understand the term. It meant essentially a form of partnership in which the natives could be accorded some right to self-administration, or to participation in government, within the existing framework of colonial bureaucracy, which left real responsibility in French hands. In administrative terms, it meant government by a Governor-General, nominated by and responsible to the government in Paris, assisted by advisory Councils on which natives were represented (usually in a minority). Parliamentary representation remained limited to those colonies which had it at the beginning of the Third Republic. It was an association characterized by French domination, both political and economic. A French critic writing after the Second World War, described it as being

'limited to minor local reforms, unlikely to arouse the enthusiasm of the masses, a purely administrative decentralization, consisting of the creation of local advisory Councils and the granting of citizenship to individuals'. '. . . Nowhere,' he went on, 'were local and communal liberties progressively organized on the model of the English in India or the Dutch in Java.'[1]

[1] Deschamps, H., *Méthodes et doctrines coloniales de la France* (Colin, 1953), pp. 172–4.

Among measures inspired by the principle of association, were the establishment in 1900 of the Algerian *délégations financières*, providing for some degree of financial autonomy, the increase, from 1919 onwards of native representation in local Assemblies in Algeria, the retention in the two North African Protectorates of a formal native government, and the attempts by Lyautey to preserve native customs in Morocco, on both national and local levels.

Effective power remained, of course, in the hands of the French government and French interests were dominant in the economic as well as in the political sphere. In North Africa, France encouraged the settlement of French citizens and the investment of French capital made possible large-scale exploitation of the agricultural and mineral resources of the territories. In 1881 there were only 376,000 *colons* in Algeria; by 1911, the number had doubled. The cultivation of cereals, wine, olives and the mining of iron and phosphates led to a rapidly expanding trade, mainly with France. In the years preceding the Second World War, over 80 per cent of Algerian exports and about half of Tunisian and Moroccan exports went to France. The 'old colonies' sent over 90 per cent of their exports to France and some two-thirds of their imports came from France. The share of the colonies in the trade of the mother country was greater in the case of France than of any other colonial system, amounting in 1937–8 to over a quarter of France's total foreign trade.

France depended on her overseas possessions, not only to supplement her own production and to provide a market for her exports, but also to provide reserves of manpower. The colonial populations were liable for military service. During the First World War, the Empire contributed upwards of 500,000 men to the armed forces and some five million tons of goods. In addition, more than 150,000 overseas workers served in France.

There was, however, another side to the picture. If there was relatively little political evolution, there was visible social progress. 'Every station', says the critic quoted above, 'had at least its dispensary and its schools.'[1] Statistics bear witness to the effectiveness of French public health services. In Algeria, the native population more than doubled between 1872 and 1911; during the years between the two wars, the Moroccan population doubled and the population of Indo-China almost doubled. But the improvement in public health and education brought new problems. The spectacular rise in the population of North Africa meant that population was in danger of outstripping productive capacity. The provision of schools led to the growth of an educated French-speaking native *élite*, whose natural political aspirations had no adequate outlets. With economic development there came economic crises, the growth of a native proletariat, vulnerable not only to nationalist but also to communist propaganda. Repressive measures —restrictions on the right of association and public meeting, press censorship—increased the discontent and frustration of the native populations. In time, French settlers came to constitute privileged vested interests, opposed to the political and economic rights claimed by the native nationalist movements. By 1939, all the elements of a head-on clash between French and settler interests on the one hand, and native nationalism on the other, were already present.

The birth of the French Union. The events of the war years strengthened native nationalism in several ways. France's defeat, occupation and virtual separation from

[1] Deschamps, op. cit., p. 175.

her colonies reduced both her prestige and her authority. The British occupation of Syria and Madagascar and the American occupation of North Africa brought the native populations into contact with different colonial policies and attitudes, and the growth of Arab nationalism naturally influenced nationalist movements among the Muslim populations of North Africa. The provisional governments of post-war France were predominantly left-wing and therefore favourable in principle to nationalist aspirations and anxious for a new approach to colonialism, based on free co-operation and real association.

The result was the beginning of a third phase of French colonial policy. In 1946, the constitution of the Fourth Republic, drawn up by an Assembly which included over sixty representatives of the overseas territories, created the French Union.

The French Union differed from the pre-war Empire in four important respects. First, the word 'colonies' officially disappeared from the French political vocabulary. *La France d'Outre-Mer* (Overseas France) consists today of overseas possessions classified in four[1] distinct categories.[2] These are Algeria, the four overseas *départements* (the former 'old colonies'), the Overseas Territories (the former colonies), and the Associated Territories (now held in trusteeship for the United Nations). Secondly, the pre-war distinction between French citizens and native subjects has officially disappeared. All members of the Union have henceforth the constitutional status of French citizens (*la qualité de citoyen*). As such, they can claim the individual rights

[1] The former Protectorates originally constituted a fifth category, the Associated States, but all of these had become independent by 1955.
[2] The New Hebrides does not form part of the Union, being an Anglo-French Condominium.

11

guaranteed by the constitution, including the right to be represented in the parliament of the mother country and the right to vote 'in conditions to be laid down in subsequent legislation'. (It will be remembered that electoral conditions were expressly excluded from the constitution and left to be dealt with by ordinary legislation.) In practice, the suffrage rights of the native populations were restricted though the franchise increased enormously with each election. In 1946, the overseas electorate (including Europeans, but excluding Algeria) numbered one and three-quarter million, in 1951, five and a half million; in 1956, almost ten million, of whom 58 per cent actually voted. A law of June 1956 instituted the single electoral college in all overseas territories, and universal suffrage for both sexes; a law of February 1958 did the same for Algeria.[1]

In all, 82 deputies and 64 senators represent overseas territorial constituencies. They included in 1958:

(a) deputies. 30 representing Algeria (seats temporarily vacant).

10 representing the four *départements d'outre-mer* of Guadeloupe, Martinique and Réunion (3 each) and Guyana (1).

37 representing the Overseas Territories of West Africa (20), Equatorial Africa (7), Madagascar (5), St. Pierre-et-Miquelon, Somaliland, New Caledonia, the Comoro archipelago and French Oceania (1 each).

[1] The *loi-cadre* of 23 June 1956, and that of 6 February 1958. In the case of the latter, governmental statements made it plain that regional and constituency boundaries would be drawn in such a way as to give the European element considerably greater representation than strict proportionality would warrant.

5 representing the Associated Territories of the Cameroons (4) and Togoland (1).

(b) senators. 14 representing Algeria.

7 representing the four *départements d'outre-mer* of Guadeloupe, Martinique and Réunion (2 each) and Guyana (1).

38 representing the Overseas Territories of West Africa (20), Equatorial Africa (8), Madagascar (5), St. Pierre-et-Miquelon, Somaliland, New Caledonia, the Comoro archipelago and French Oceania (1 each).

5 representing the Associated Territories of the Cameroons (3) and Togoland (2).

The creation of an Assembly and a High Council of the Union constituted the third major innovation of the Union. The former, which sits at Versailles during sessions of the French parliament, began its work at the end of 1947. It may include up to 240 members, elected for six years, of whom half must always represent the mother country and half the overseas and associated territories.[1]

The functions of the Assembly of the Union are advisory only. It is consulted regarding the application

[1] French representatives are nominated by the Assembly and the Council of the Republic (which nominates two-thirds and one-third respectively from outside their own ranks); overseas councillors are elected by the territorial Assemblies. After the 1953 elections, overseas representation was as follows: *départements d'outre-mer*, 4; Algeria, 18 (of whom 6 represent the Saharan regions); Overseas Territories, 47. Of the former Associated States only Laos still wished to send representatives in 1957.

of legislation to overseas territories and regarding Presidential decrees applicable to them, as well as on the determination of (or any proposed change in) the status of the territory. It may, in addition, recommend the introduction of legislation affecting the overseas territories. The functions of the High Council are described in the constitution as being 'to assist the government in the conduct of the affairs of the Union' and it was presumably intended to be a co-ordinating body. It was composed of a French delegation and of delegations from each member Associated State and was presided over *ex officio* by the President of the Republic. It met only three times, and by the end of 1953 was virtually dead. The North African Protectorates refused to accept the status of Associated States, and also refused to be represented in either the Assembly of the Union or the High Council. The Assembly of the Union after the 1953 elections included, therefore, only 204 members out of a permitted 240.

The fourth innovation of the Union was the implementation of the French undertaking (in the preamble of the constitution and in the United Nations Charter) to lead the people in her care towards free and democratic self-administration. This did not mean that France had adopted the goal of self-government for the former colonies. It meant rather that she was prepared to accept an extension of native rights along lines similar to those adopted in application of the principle of association. The meeting of colonial Governors and officials, held in Brazzaville in 1944, expressed clearly what was, no doubt, the opinion of most Frenchmen:

'The goal of France's civilizing work in the colonies', says the report, 'does not include autonomy.

Any evolution leading to separation from the family of the French Empire is ruled out, as is the setting-up, even in the far distant future, of systems of self-government in the Colonies.'[1]

As an immediate application of the undertaking to extend native political rights, local representative Assemblies were set up in 1947 and 1948 in all overseas territories. These Assemblies were elected for five years by all those whose names were on the electoral register. Their numbers varied in number according to the population of the territory, African and Madagascan Assemblies including from thirty to fifty. Voting was at first in two separate colleges but, once elected, councillors sat together. West and Equatorial African Federations possessed, in addition, Grand Councils, and Madagascar a Representative Council for the whole island, whose members are elected by the territorial Assemblies. These Assemblies were intended to assist the Governor in the administration of the territory. They had the right to be consulted regarding proposals to change the status of the territory, and they were intended also to act as a training-ground for native politicians and so to enable the native populations to play an increasingly important part in the running of affairs, both in their own countries and, indirectly, in Paris. For the territorial Assemblies are also the electoral colleges for overseas senators as well as for overseas members of the Assembly of the Union. Their functions were greatly extended in 1956.

---

[1] cf. the expression used in the preamble to the constitution; 'la liberté de s'administrer eux-mêmes et de gérer démocratiquement leurs propres affaires', which does not imply self-government in the British sense of the term.

THE ADMINISTRATION OF THE TERRITORIES
OF THE UNION

The administrative structure of the Union is not only more complicated than that of the pre-war Empire, but it has been in an almost continuous state of rapid evolution, owing to the growing pressure, first of nationalist movements in the far-Eastern and North African Protectorates, and later of nationalism in Algeria and emergent nationalism in the other African territories. The concept of the Union exhibited clearly the persistence of the assimilative tradition of French colonial policy. The head of the Union is the President of the Republic, elected by the French Parliament. Overseas representatives still sit—more numerous than before the war, but inevitably a minority—in the French Assemblies. There was great reluctance on the part of many Frenchmen to accede to North African demands for autonomy and much more reluctance in the case of Algeria, administered as, and considered to be, an integral part of France.

The result has been perpetual modifications of the structure though, up to 1958, no change had been made in the formal constitutional status of the Union as defined by articles 60 to 82 of the constitution. In North Africa, prolonged resistance by administrators on the spot, and by some governments, to demands for limited autonomy, failed to prevent the grant of independence to Tunisia and Morocco, in 1955. The failure of successive governments to accord to Algerian Moslems the degree of autonomy that they had been led to expect from the application of the Algerian Statute of 1947 led to a rebellion in 1954, whose leaders refused to be satisfied with anything less than independence. In the former colonies, however, the 'outline-law' of June 1956, which introduced a measure of autonomy and universal suffrage, was speedily put into effect, with the co-operation of the political leaders.

(*i*) *The 'old colonies' and Algeria.* The *départements* of Algeria and the four 'old colonies' are described officially as *départements d'outre-mer*.[1] The four *départements* of Guadeloupe, Martinique, Réunion and Guyana all have their prefects and their Departmental Councils and are administered in principle in exactly the same way as *départements* in the mother country, being, like them, subject to the control of the Ministry of the Interior. In practice, of course, legislation is adapted where necessary to the special conditions existing in these territories.[2]

Algerian administration already exhibited a number of special features before the vote, in September 1947, of the Algerian Statute. This described the territory as 'a group of *départements* enjoying . . . financial autonomy and a special organization'. Algeria had, for instance, a Governor-General, who represented the French government throughout the whole territory, and whose staff was responsible for the administration of all services except those of Justice and Education (*les services rattachés*) which were administered directly from Paris, by the appropriate Ministries. An Algerian Assembly was first elected in 1948, consisting of 120 members, one half representing European and assimilated residents, the other half the Moslem population. Its functions were to supervise financial administration, pronounce on the advisability of applying French legislation to

[1] According to a decision of the *Conseil d'Etat* of 27 March 1947.
[2] The former 'old colonies' have enjoyed this status since 1946, when a law of 19 March was passed in response to the wishes of the population. The change of status was incorporated in the 1946 constitution.

Algeria,[1] to state whether measures regarded as applicable needed adaptation, and to pronounce on the need for executive measures. It was an advisory body, whose decisions required the approbation of the French government.[2] The southern regions of Algeria, covering an area ten times the size of the *départements*, but consisting mainly of desert and with a population of under a million, remained predominantly under military jurisdiction, but the Statute provided for their eventual integration with the more evolved parts of Algeria.

The Algerian Statute was intended to accord a degree of decentralization to Algeria and to increase the effective participation of Moslems in local administration. It proved a failure, partly because French governments did not apply the sections providing for Moslem political evolution, and, partly, because with the growth of nationalism and the outbreak of the nationalist rebellion in November 1954, it rapidly ceased, even on paper, to satisfy even moderate Moslem opinion.

From the end of 1956 onwards, French governments tried to break out of the vicious circle created on the one hand by nationalist refusal to agree to a cease-fire without prior recognition of Algeria's right to independence, and on the other by French insistence that the future of Algeria could be decided only by negotiations between France and freely elected representative Moslem spokesmen. Administrative reforms were carried out, destined to provide the institutional framework within which elections could speedily be held, once the fighting had ceased.

---

[1] French legislation is applicable to the four *départements d'outre-mer*, unless the law specifies otherwise. Apart from certain matters explicitly enumerated, it is not applied to Algeria, unless specific provisions are included to that effect.
[2] The Algerian Assembly was dissolved on 12 April 1956, most of its Moslem representatives having already resigned.

First, local government was reorganized. The number of *départements* was increased from three to twelve; the less evolved *communes* (*communes mixtes*), where Moslem representatives were nominated instead of elected, were given the status of *communes de plein exercice*, which have fully elected Councils and follow the pattern of a French Municipal Council; and, until elections could be held, the newly created *communes* and the existing *communes de plein exercice* were to be administered by provisional nominated 'delegations' or commissions. Departmental Councils, too, were to have special nominated administrations. The intention was to get rid of European elements hostile to Moslem emancipation, to make a fresh start.

In February 1958, an 'outline-law' for Algeria laid down a new framework for the central administration. It was described by left-wing opinion as irrelevant, since Moslem opinion had not been consulted. It was relevant, however, in the sense that only the French Parliament was, in 1958, juridically competent to decide how Algeria should be governed.

Briefly summarized, the law provided for:

(i) regional decentralization. Algeria was to be divided into 'Territories', each enjoying a degree of self-administration,

(ii) democratically elected Territorial Assemblies (until elections could be held, the special local administrations were to nominate members),

(iii) Territorial governments responsible to these Assemblies, heads of governments being nominated by the President of the Republic,

(iv) Community Councils, with nominated members representing both European and Moslem interests,

(v) Federal organs of government, to be set up when

half the Territorial Assemblies had decided on the functions that should be delegated to federal organs; the latter to consist of an Assembly, chosen by delegates of Territorial organs, and a Council, in which Territories would have equal rights of representation.

The electoral law, voted at the same time as the 'outline-law', was even more of an outline, leaving crucial questions such as boundary delimitation to be worked out later. The important thing about it was that it did away with the double college.[1]

The discovery of oil in the Sahara led to an important administrative change at the end of 1956, which affected the southern regions of Algeria, three West and one Equatorial African Territory. A law of 29 December set up a Common Organization for the Saharan Regions of these Territories, for the purpose of developing their economic resources and increasing the standards of living of the populations. The government formed in June 1957 included for the first time a Minister for the Saharan regions.

The Organization, which comprised a representative of the government of the Republic, a Technical Committee and a High Commission of thirty-two members, of whom half represented the four constitutional Assemblies of the Republic and half the populations of the Saharan regions (eight representing Algeria) met for the first time in January 1958. Its function was to co-ordinate and supervise the application of development programmes.

(*ii*) *The Overseas Territories and the Associated*

[1] It should be pointed out that boundary delimitation could (and according to the Minister Residing in Algeria would be designed to) prevent one Moslem vote having the same electoral value as one European vote.

Territories. The administration of the remaining former colonies, now called *Territoires d'Outre-Mer*, is the responsibility of the Ministry for Overseas France, formerly called the Ministry for the Colonies. These comprise both unitary administrations (the Comoro archipelago and Oceania, Somaliland, New Caledonia, and St. Pierre-et-Miquelon) and Federations (the West and Equatorial African Federations). The Madagascan system is classed as unitary, although divided for administration purposes into five provinces.

Before the reforms of 1956 and 1957, the Associated Territories were administered (in accordance with the rules of the Trusteeship Council) to all intents and purposes as if they formed part of the Union and so were also the responsibility of the Ministry for Overseas France. There were certain formal differences—such as, for instance, the obligation on the part of France to furnish reports on her administration to the Trusteeship Council and the prohibition of compulsory military service[1]—but in all essential respects the administration was similar to that of territories within the Union. Illogically, perhaps, since the inhabitants of these territories are not French, they had the status of citizens of the Union and elected representatives to the French parliament. This has been defended on the ground that they were international, and therefore without a government of their own, by virtue of a decision in which they had no voice. According to this view, they should, therefore, in a democratic system, be accorded the right of expressing their points of view and of participating in the governmental process.

Up to 1956, the Overseas and Associated Territories had roughly similar patterns of administration. There

[1] France had the right, however, to raise volunteer contingents.

was a representative of the French government, a Governor or Commissioner of the Republic and a Governor-General in the Federations and Madagascar, responsible to the government in Paris for the administration of the territory and for its defence. He was assisted by an advisory Council comprising the heads of the different services and selected native leaders, and by the elected Assemblies whose composition and functions have already been described. The French parliament legislated for the Overseas Territories and, indeed, had sole say in matters concerning criminal legislation, political or administrative organization and individual rights. In other matters, parliament reserved the right to apply legislation to these territories, either by legislative enactment or by decree. In the former case, the Assembly of the Union *might* be consulted; in the latter case, the constitution requires that it *should* be consulted. In addition, the government issued decrees applicable directly to individual territories. In such cases, the decree was signed by the President of the Republic after consultation with the Assembly of the Union. Nothing, either in the constitution or in French practice, bound the government to follow the advice proffered by the Assembly of the Union. The extent to which colonial opinion was taken into account depended, therefore, entirely on one or more of three things; on the attitude of the French government, or that of the French parliament, and on the spirit in which the Governor, as the French government's representative on the spot, interpreted the decree of 25 October 1946 requiring him to consult the local Assembly before issuing the orders which he was entitled to make in application of French laws or decrees.

From 1956 onwards, great changes were made in the

administration of the Overseas and Associated Territories. At the end of the year, Togoland became an
'autonomous republic' within the French Union, with
an Assembly elected for five years by universal suffrage,
a government responsible to the Assembly, and a Prime
Minister chosen by a procedure similar to that by which
Prime Ministers are chosen in France. The High
Commissioner, representing the French Republic,
occupies the position of Head of the State.

In 1957, a similar constitution for the Cameroons was
approved by the French Parliament, though, in this case,
autonomy is as yet less complete. France retains control
of foreign policy, defence, finance, justice and questions
concerning civil liberties.

In June 1956 an 'outline-law' created three major
changes in the administration of the Overseas Territories
which amounted to the grant of semi-autonomy. The
first extends the powers of the Territorial Assemblies.
In future these will manage their own affairs, except for
essential services for which France retains responsibility,
in particular those concerned with foreign affairs, defence,
the army, finance, communications, civil liberties, the
maintenance of security and higher education. The list
is admittedly long, but it must be remembered that many
of these Territories are still politically very backward
and have had only a few years' experience of the working
of representative government.

The second change was the setting-up of appropriate
organs of government to exercise the newly granted
powers. The general pattern is similar to that of the
governments of Togoland and the Cameroons, with a
French official as Head of the Territory and President of the governmental Council—which is, in effect,
an embryo cabinet, whose members, elected by the

Territorial Assemblies, are called Ministers; and a Vice-President who acts as Prime Minister. This post is held by the Minister who heads the poll. The governmental Council is not responsible to the Assembly, though some African leaders are anxious that it should be; but governments *may* resign if they feel they no longer have the confidence of the Assembly. If a parliamentary system of government is to develop, this will mean, in fact, that governments will, sooner or later, become responsible *de jure*, as they will no doubt now be responsible *de facto*.

The third change was the introduction of universal suffrage, for men and women alike, throughout the Overseas Territories. The first elections held on that basis took place in March 1957, when Territorial Assemblies were elected in eighteen Territories of Africa and in Madagascar.

There were signs during 1957 of growing pains as the new institutions began to function. Some native leaders wanted to move faster than others, and, while some were thinking in terms of the ultimate autonomy of the Territories within the French Union, others were in favour of large federal groupings, related to the mother country also by federal links. What was encouraging to France, however, was first, the victory of moderate nationalist elements in the elections, and, second, the very large majorities by which both Togoland and the Cameroons voted to remain within the framework of the French Union.

If the first decade of the French Union's existence was one of increasing strain and difficulty between France and the former Protectorates, the second decade at least began with the prospect of a more fruitful co-operation between France and her Overseas Territories.

PART II

The Post-war Political Scene

*

CHAPTER VIII

INTERNAL PROBLEMS

The progress of reconstruction. There seems at first sight to be a contradiction between the speed with which the French were able to restore the economic machine to normal running order, and the recurrent signs during the post-war years, both of serious economic disequilibrium and of social and industrial unrest. Destruction during the Second World War was much more extensive than during the First World War, and economic dislocation also was much greater. Machinery had been worn out, stocks depleted, fields sown with mines. Nearly two million men had been in captivity and many more forced to work, either in France or in Germany, for the German war effort; many more had left their homes and occupations to work in the resistance movement. When the war ended, French overseas trade was virtually at a standstill, two-thirds of the merchant navy destroyed, over half of the ports out of action. Internal communications were almost non-existent. Two-thirds of the railway track, over half the large marshalling yards and 9,000 bridges were unusable. Production of coal and of steel had fallen from 48 and 6 million tons in 1938 to 35 and $1\frac{1}{2}$ million tons respectively.

These figures do not really begin to describe the immensity of the task of reconstruction with which post-war France has been faced. But, in spite of all the difficulties, in spite of the shortage of food, materials, manpower, and the disorganization of essential services, by 1948 French production was almost back to normal. By 1950, both agricultural and industrial production were above the 1938 level, and the following year, the general level of production was even slightly above that of 1929, previously the record year.

The political and social climate. In spite of this achievement, in spite, too, of France's relatively abundant home production of food, not a year passed from 1947 to 1953 without either wide-spread strikes or one or more government crises, caused by economic issues. In the autumn of 1947, there were strikes, mainly among engineering workers, miners, railways workers and state employees, involving upwards of two or more million men; the following year, there was a national mining strike and sympathetic strikes by railwaymen, dockers, and some steel workers; in the autumn of 1949, there was a government crisis which lasted three weeks; in the spring of 1950 and again in 1951, there were more strikes, mainly among dockers and engineering workers; at the end of 1951, a budgetary crisis brought down the government in the first week of the new year; and at the end of 1952 the government resigned owing to difficulties over the next year's budget; in 1953, there was a governmental interregnum of over five weeks, a record for both Third and Fourth Republics, and a three weeks' strike of the transport services disorganized holiday traffic for most of August.

The most important single cause of the strikes was the rise in the cost of living. Except for a brief interval in 1949, prices rose steadily from the end of the war to 1952. The general price index which at the end of 1946 had been between eight and nine times that of 1938, was eighteen times as high at the end of 1949.

In 1953, prices were 45 per cent higher than they had been in 1949, and French prices were then from 15 to 20 per cent higher than world prices.

Wages rose too, of course, but the continual readjustments always followed the movement of prices, without ever catching it up.[1] The trade unions could, and did, argue that the wage- and salary-earning classes were the chief victims of a continuous inflation, which was benefiting certain sections of the community, in particular some of the farmers and the larger industrialists. In 1951, the purchasing power of wage-earning classes was actually lower than it had been in 1938. In both England and Belgium real wages had risen considerably.

The nature of French post-war problems. There are both economic and political explanations of this state of affairs. The very magnitude and diversity of the economic demands made on the post-war French state would have imposed almost unbearable stresses and strains on more stable economies. The extent to which France was unable to meet them helped to show up long-standing weaknesses of her economic organization, pointing to the urgent need of a radical overhaul of the whole system. A beginning was made with the application of the first Monnet Plan for the modernization and re-equipment of six basic industries. But, in spite of the successful completion of the four-year plan, it was clear

[1] In 1950 the retail price index stood at 2,000 (1938 = 100), the wage index, based on the average wage of an unskilled engineering worker in the Paris region, at 1,000 (1939 = 100) (André Bisson, *L'Inflation française* (Recueil Sirey), 1953, p. 57). This is not an accurate indication of the average gap between wages and prices, however, as the wage index related only to unskilled workers. Allowance must also be made, in trying to assess the rise in the cost of living, for the low level of rents, which was some compensation for the high cost of food. When all allowances have been made, the gap remained considerable for the lower-paid workers.

12

by the end of 1952 that its achievement had left the root of the problem untouched. Successive French governments were unable to do more than scratch the surface, owing to the pressure of events, the inadequacy of French resources and the profound political divisions on economic policy, as on almost everything else.

The most striking characteristic of French post-war internal politics is the way in which economic and political preoccupations have reacted on each other, together with the consequent confusion of mind and multiplication of obstacles to the solution of problems in both fields. In so far as French economic problems were capable of solution, either by individual effort, or by governmental action acceptable by and large to the political parties, economic recovery progressed. But traditional ways and stop-gap policies could not do more than put the clock back to 1938, or, at most, and with a great effort, to 1929. The rate of French agricultural and industrial progress had been falling off in relation to that of other European countries since 1929, and comparisons with 1938, while they constituted a tribute to the speed and energy with which post-war France had got back to normal, afforded no guide to the extent to which she was equipped to take her place in post-war Europe. M. Monnet's analysis of French economic conditions in 1946 had led him to the conclusion that she was faced with the alternatives of modernization or decadence. In 1953, even after the successful modernization of some of the most important basic industries, statesmen whose politics were as different as those of M. Reynaud and M. Mendès-France were agreed that:

'France's position is one of continued regression, as far as world competition is concerned. Since 1929,

American production has doubled, in Great Britain and Western Germany it has increased by 50 per cent. Ours has increased by only 8 per cent. Germany can build 437,000 housing units in the time it takes us to build 80,000.'[1]

'The fundamental cause of all the ills that afflict the country,' said M. Mendès-France, 'is the multiplicity and the scope of the tasks which have been undertaken at one and the same time; reconstruction, modernization and equipment, the development of overseas territories, the improvement of the standard of living and the introduction of social reforms, the development of exports, the war in Indo-China, the building up of a strong and powerful army in Europe . . . etc. Events have confirmed the conclusion that could have been reached by reflection, namely, that one cannot do everything at once. Government means choice, however difficult the choice may be.'[2]

It certainly proved, in fact, impossible to choose. The example of housing, quoted above, illustrates very clearly the difficulties with which governments were faced. The housing record was admittedly one of the black spots in post-war reconstruction. But the problem was one which post-war France had inherited from the previous post-war period. True, it had been aggravated by the destruction of the Second World War. But, during the whole of the relatively prosperous inter-war period, France had built only 1,800,000 housing units,

[1] Mendès-France, P., *Gouverner, c'est choisir* (La Nef-Julliard, 1953), p. 18. The passage, quoted by M. Mendès-France in his investiture speech, is a quotation from the speech made by M. Reynaud a few days earlier.
[2] Ibid., p. 20.

compared with a British production, which, at its peak, reached 300,000 a year, with a total construction of three and a half million. In 1939, France was already one of the worst housed countries in Europe. An out-of-date rent system had succeeded in discouraging private building and the state had been either unable or unwilling to fill the gap. In the second post-war period, it was the appalling housing shortage, as much as the ever-rising price level indicative of the general inadequacy of economic resources or economic policies, which created working-class discontent, encouraged communism, and so helped to make the political deadlock more complete.

The economic deadlock. The economic problems were in themselves sufficiently intractable even if there had been no political problem. Governments were faced with too many demands, all apparently equally urgent, but not all either physically compatible or materially possible, given the available resources. The reconstruction and reorganization achieved owed a great deal to American aid—first to the loan, negotiated in 1946 by Léon Blum, and then to Marshall Aid. But the demands were substantially increased by the cost of the war in Indo-China and by the stepping up of the rearmament programme, following the outbreak of the war in Korea. By 1953, military expenditure accounted for almost a third of French annual expenditure, and a third of that total was required to continue the Indo-Chinese war, in spite of greatly increased supplies of war materials from the United States from the beginning of 1951. Nor was any end of the war then in sight.

The combined effect of pressure from all sides on a budget continually and increasingly in deficit was that, by 1953, the cry, 'We cannot do everything at once' was becoming increasingly insistent. Either something had to go, or France would have to find new ways of meeting her increasingly heavy commitments.

What happened was that, in June 1954, M. Mendès-France came on the scene and, for six months, a French government gave the impression that it knew where it wanted to go and how to get there. With the Geneva settlement, the defeat of E.D.C., the formation of Western European Union, the apparent settlement of the German problem, and the opening of negotiations for the independence of Tunisia, most of the problems that had bedevilled previous governments and given rise to the *immobilisme* characteristic of post-war French politics, seemed to have disappeared. By the end of 1954, M. Mendès-France was ready to tackle what had always been in his view the major problem impeding France's recovery of her rightful place in the world, namely, her economic backwardness.

He was not allowed to do more than make a start, however. Deputies who had swallowed the humiliation of the loss of Indo-China and Tunisian independence, as the only way out of an intolerable deadlock, had recovered some of their buoyancy by the end of the year. There was far more opposition to any suggestion of a change in the status of Algeria, where the rebellion had just broken out. And M. Mendès-France's unpopularity with the Right had been further increased by his attack on the vested interests of distillers and beetroot producers.

The need for economic modernization had been publicized by economists and financial experts from 1953 onwards. In 1953 the Economic and Financial Services of the Ministry of Finance presented to a newly constituted Committee of Accounts, representing the two houses of parliament, the two advisory chambers and a number of economic experts and high officials of the different government departments, a report on French public accounts, drawing attention to some of the causes of these problems. The facts enumerated certainly constituted a formidable indictment. But even if they were generally accepted as providing an accurate picture of the situation, they threw no light on the vital problem, which was how that situation could be changed in the near future, without involving an upheaval as drastic as the French Revolution.

A brief summary of some of the facts quoted in the report will be sufficient to indicate the scope of the problem. French agriculture, it was stated, was badly organized and under-productive. There were too many small and scattered farms employing either no labour outside that of the family or only one or two workers. Of the total area under wheat cultivation, 6 per cent was uneconomic, 22 per cent was barely economic, thanks to the expenditure of an excessive amount of labour. The general standard of living of farmers was low, and many made a living only thanks to state subsidies, tax exemptions and tax evasion. Industrial production was increasing at a slower rate in France than in other European countries, and productivity was actually increasing at a slower rate than before the war, largely owing to inefficient methods, lack of modern equipment and insufficient utilization of power. Here again, there were too many small concerns, employing only from one to five workers. These constituted, in 1950, over 70 per cent of the total number of industrial establishments. The result was high costs and high prices. Economic stagnation was encouraged by a network of restrictive practices throughout the productive and distributive systems. Prices tended to be fixed at levels that enabled inefficient concerns to survive and so enabled the more efficient concerns to make high profits. The inefficient could not increase production, since they lacked the necessary capital resources; the efficient had no incentive to do so when high profits could be made with restricted production and little effort. There were too many small retail traders and their number was increasing. Both small producers and small traders were often compelled to resort to systematic tax evasion, in order to survive. The estimated loss to the revenue was of the order of 20 per cent in the case of producers and 28 per cent in the case of distributors.[1]

What this amounted to was the criticism that, in the French economic system, the instincts of individual thrift and calculation, characteristic of capitalism, were present, without its drive, initiative and enterprise. There had been sufficient distrust of the state to prevent controls from working efficiently in the interests of the consumer, but there was sufficient distrust of individual enterprise to allow farmers, industrialists and traders to call for state controls (and to supplement them with private arrangements) in the interests of the producer. One result was that governments, compelled to raise revenue from somewhere, had to rely largely on indirect taxes. These were unjust, not only because they were regressive, but because they were often passed on from producer to consumer. In addition, an unfair share of direct taxation was paid by wage and salary earners

[1] *Rapports du Service des Etudes économiques et financières du Ministère des Finances sur les Comptes provisoires de la nation des années 1951 et 1952* (Paris, Imprimerie Nationale, 1953), pp. 40–79.

who had their taxes deducted at source, and so could not evade their obligations.

One of the remedies constantly suggested was a complete overhaul of the fiscal system, in order to render it both more equitable and more efficient. This proved impossible of achievement partly because, even if the reforms had been agreed on, they would have taken years to carry out, but also because the political obstacles proved insuperable.

The political deadlock. Three post-war circumstances contributed to produce political deadlock; first, the distribution of party strengths in the Assembly and left-wing differences on doctrinal matters; second, the intractability in themselves of many post-war problems and the consequent acute differences between and within parties; and third, the existence from 1951 onwards, of two different and irreconcilable oppositions in the Assembly, at first Communists and Gaullists and, from 1956, Communists and extreme Right.

In 1945, nothing looked less likely than a numerical deadlock, and yet the trouble really started then. The large majority enjoyed by the three left-wing parties at the 1945 elections enabled them to introduce, almost without opposition, a number of measures for the nationalization of industries. They had been able to agree on the general lines of economic policy. They were not agreed on a number of constitutional points. And so, for a year, while the new constitution was being hammered out, they aired their differences publicly. And they did so in an atmosphere which can only be described as a perpetual election campaign. For during that year there were two constitutional referenda and two general elections, and the three parties, having been returned in 1945 in virtually equal numbers, were far more conscious of their electoral rivalry than of their governmental partnership. By 1947, when the need for co-operation between the democratic parties became imperative, in order to combat the challenge of communism on the Left and Gaullism on the Right, the psychological opportunity for more constructive co-operation had been lost.

In the 1951 Assembly, although the need for co-operation between the democratic parties was no less imperative, a hexagon of parties proved incapable of providing governments with either consistent or clear majorities. The result of virtual numerical equality between parties normally supporting the government and those normally voting with the opposition was to increase the power of pressure groups. It was difficult enough for governments to muster the necessary parliamentary support for matters that required immediate decisions, such as the voting of the budget, or the determination of the French attitude to international issues as they arose. Action on more controversial or far-reaching matters was out of the question. Since a handful of rebels could defeat a government, the marginal member of a parliamentary group acquired a vital importance, and since the right-wing and radical parties are loosely organized and their members, in general, allergic to party discipline, the marginal member was most likely to be a member of one of these groups. He was, more often than not, a representative of precisely those elements most resistant to change, of the small farmer, winegrower or business man, whose interests were threatened by proposals for a more rational organization of the French economic system and a more equitable system of taxation. Thus, for instance, one of the difficulties that led to the resignation of M. Pinay in December 1952

176   FRANCE: THE FOURTH REPUBLIC

was the hostility of many of his own supporters to his proposals for tax reform.[1] The difficulties that socialists, members of the MRP and radicals experienced in trying to work together were increased by the extent to which their differences cut across the normal frontiers separating Left and Right in French politics. In the pre-war Chamber of Deputies, parties were, as M. Siegfried has shown, relatively easily classifiable as belonging either to the Right or to the Left. The radicals, as an anti-clerical party, belonged to the Left. Catholics, with the exception of a handful of progressives, were normally classed as being on the Right. In the post-war Assembly, the divisions between the different parties were much more complex. They were, indeed, trebly tripartite. 'Never', said M. Fauvet, 'do three neighbouring parties find themselves on the same side of three great dividing lines. That is the sole cause of the instability of majorities, even of the régime.'[2]

It is perhaps too much to say that these dividing lines constituted the sole cause of instability, but certainly they helped to create and perpetuate it. The three dividing lines were, of course, the religious-cum-educational issue, economic and social policy, and the principle of political democracy. On the first, socialists and communists favoured a purely secular system of state-controlled education and opposed any state aid, either for catholic schools or for catholic parents, if the purpose

[1] It is only fair to state that this was not the immediate cause of M. Pinay's resignation. M. Guy Petit, a member of his government and a prominent member of the peasant group which in general supported M. Pinay, stated, however, in October at the group's annual congress that M. Pinay had against him 'all the economic and social vested interests, as well as all the feudal corporations in the land'.

[2] op. cit., p. 264.

of the aid was to assist them to educate their children in catholic schools. The MRP, the RPF and most of the right-wing members were favourable to catholicism. The radicals remained anti-clerical, but were more prepared to compromise than were the two other anti-clerical parties. On economic and social policy, communists were whole-hearted collectivist planners; socialists and, to a lesser extent, MRP, were democratic planners; all the other parties believed in theory in the traditional methods of free enterprise and in practice in the restrictive devices with which vested interests had impeded its effective working. On the third issue, communists were totalitarian, believing in the system described variously as 'popular democracy', 'democratic centralism' and 'the dictatorship of the proletariat'; the RPF wanted strong government and was prepared to reform the constitution drastically in order to get it; the other parties wanted to retain the present form of parliamentary democracy, even at the cost of weak government (though they differed on the extent of the need for constitutional reforms).

Of the three conceptions concerning the régime, parliamentary democracy alone had the support of the majority of members in the Assembly. But governments constituted on that basis did not necessarily have a majority on issues involving religion and economics. And both have bedevilled post-war French politics.

The result of this complexity of divisions on different issues was to create a situation in which, only too often, a majority could be found in the Assembly only to oppose. To quote only one example, M. Pleven was defeated at the beginning of 1952, because the socialists (whose support or neutrality was in practice necessary for the survival of the government) voted against his proposal to investigate the running of the nationalized industries; his successor, M. Faure, was defeated a month or so later, because the Right and some of the radicals (whose support was necessary for *his* survival) opposed his proposal for increased taxation; M. Pinay's resignation, ten months later, was due to the opposition of the Right to tax reform and that of the Left (in this case the MRP) to his decision not to increase family allowances. In all these cases, the merits of the different proposals were to some extent obscured by party or doctrinal stands on principle. They added up to successive refusals on the part of the Assembly to balance the budget, either by cutting expenditure or by providing additional revenue. Since the Assembly was divided differently on the different issues, the conclusions did not add up to any positive policy. 'There is not *a* majority,' said M. Fauvet in May 1953, 'there are different majorities on different issues.'[1]

No doubt it is possible to govern for a time with shifting majorities (*des majorités de rechange*), provided that issues are not so passionately contested that the partisans of one view consider the fall of the government a lesser evil than their own defeat, or, as more usually happened, provided that some sort of face-saving formula can be worked out which avoids defeat for either side. In so far as this could be achieved, the result was usually that the government was prevented in practice from doing anything and the problem was shelved for the time being. Government is much more difficult when there are different majorities in the Assembly on foreign and domestic policies, as happened during the E.D.C. controversy, or, as happened repeatedly over North Africa,

[1] *Le Monde*, 30.5.53.

when there is no majority at all for any constructive policy.

By 1956, the Algerian rebellion, which had begun in the Aurès mountains at the end of 1954, had produced a fourfold deadlock, which threatened during the next two years more disastrous political consequences than any of the other problems that had bedevilled post-war French Assemblies and governments. It was a military deadlock, to which few, outside official circles in Algeria, could see any speedy end; it was an economic deadlock, the cost in money, men and resources involving budgetary dislocation and social friction, and threatening the future of the economic modernization programme; it was an international deadlock, since it inevitably affected the relations of the Western Powers with the whole Arab world; and it was a political problem, since the parties were so divided that Governments were powerless.

The passage of the 'outline-law' for Algeria, in February 1958, provides a striking illustration of this. As finally voted, its provisions were somewhat less liberal than those of the text which had been rejected by the Assembly the previous September, bringing about a fall of the government. Nobody was under the illusion that Moslem opinion (if it had been consulted) would have accepted the first text, much less the second. But concessions had to be made to right-wing opinion in the Assembly in order to get the bill voted and to ensure the survival of the Government, irrespective of whether what was being voted was contributing to the solution of the problem or the perpetuation of the deadlock. For, as M. Edgar Faure pointed out at the time, what really mattered, if the problem were to be solved, was not to convince the *Indépendants*, but to convince the Moslems.

The third cause of political and parliamentary dead-lock, namely, the presence in the Assembly, from 1956 onwards, of a permanent opposition, amounting to almost a third of the membership of the Assembly, whose constituent elements disliked each other more than they disliked Governments, was a consequence of previous deadlocks as much as a cause of fresh ones. For it was, in part, though only in part, a manifestation of the growing dissatisfaction of the public with the working of democratic parliamentary government in France.

Can the deadlock be broken? A number of different suggestions have been put forward at one time or another in the hope that they might provide a solution for France's political deadlock. One is the abandonment of the system of proportional representation. No doubt, in so far as proportional representation is an accurate reflection of a much divided opinion, it helps to perpetuate deadlock by reflecting it. But France is not the only country to have a multi-party system and pro-portional representation. That is the rule in European countries. It is Great Britain which constitutes the exception. Other countries (notably Holland, which, incidentally, has her own religious problem) achieve more stable government, while French governments were no more stable between 1928 and 1939 when France did not have proportional representation. It is possible to argue that the system that she had at that time (*le scrutin d'arrondissement à deux tours*, or single-member system with two ballots) had its own weaknesses. It is equally possible—and France's long history of elec-toral experiments would seem to justify the view—that the electoral system merely reflects a disequilibrium whose causes are more deep-seated. In fact, under the 1951 electoral law, proportional representation was distorted and largely abandoned in most constituencies, without any sign of a change in the electoral habits often attributed to the existence of proportional representation.

A suggestion put forward by politicians of the Right and Centre is easier dissolution, in the hope that the electorate will provide a solution, when governments are faced with an ungovernable Assembly, or that the threat of dissolution will make deputies more amenable to discipline. It is difficult to see how this would help matters, in the absence of changes both in the electoral system and in French electoral habits. A dissolution followed by a general election can enable the elector to choose between *two* policies. But how does it help him to choose between a number of possible group permutations, if he can vote only for one group, and without knowing the conditions which will prevail when that group has to negotiate with the others? As parties conduct elections, at present, there is nothing, or very little, to help the elector in one constituency to know how his actions will affect the fortunes of another, let alone how they will affect the fortunes of his party on the national level. For a dissolution to be effective, he would need to be able to choose between national policies drawn up by coalitions of groups, constituting an approximation to a government and an opposition. The result of the 1955 dissolution was that the elections merely resulted in the mixture as before—or worse.

There have been signs for some time of attempts to find methods that would make possible the emergence of something equivalent to the British system, in which a government majority faces a coherent opposition. In the 1956 election, Socialists and *Mendésiste* radicals fought in alliance on a common programme, but the agreement barely survived the elections. The Republican Front was really no more than an electoral front.

The advantages of some such development are obvious, of course, but the obstacles to any such regrouping in the near future are much greater than is often realized. To many British observers, the habit of compromise is so deeply ingrained that they tend to regard it as a normal expression of political good sense, rather than as the kind of behaviour which is made possible by a special set of circumstances. Frenchmen, familiar with the particular difficulties of their own situation, do not always succeed in conveying to outsiders exactly how and why these difficulties prevent the kind of action that British critics recommend. For example, M. Goguel's analysis of the triple *tripartisme* of French political divisions, while it helps to explain *how* French parties behave, does not always make it clear (at least to British readers) *why* French parties apparently choose to go on differing to the point of depriving themselves, along with their opponents, of even half a loaf. The British student of French politics is left with an uneasy question at the back of his mind. Are these difficulties really insuperable, or are they an excuse for what is really unwillingness to compromise?

The answer to the question is, surely, that the obstacles to co-operation are sometimes so great that the dividing line between unwillingness and inability is difficult to draw. There are a number of major obstacles to the speedy achievement of anything in the nature, on the one hand of a government coalition with a full sense of collective responsibility, and on the other of an organized and coherent opposition. The first is the lack of either a tradition of compromise or the machinery for it. The relation between the parliamentary representative and his electors is one that grows up gradually, and traditions, once established, are difficult to change, except perhaps under the stimulus of some great national emergency. It is the tragedy of France, and to a lesser extent of other European countries as well, not excluding Great Britain, that the electors and their representatives find economic and political dangers less easy to recognize than military. France's long tradition of political instability increases her difficulty. Familiarity breeds contempt, and it is not always easy to recognize the point at which instability ceases to be merely a national inconvenience and becomes an international problem.

The machinery of compromise is bound to be both more difficult to operate and less effective in a multi-party system like the French than in a two-party system like the British. In Great Britain, the elector is voting for a party and a programme, and only incidentally for a member of parliament. But in France, the elector is voting in the first place for an individual and not even incidentally for a government or a governmental programme. For neither the elector nor the deputy knows how the government will be constituted or what will be its policy. But both know that their party's chances of having a greater or a lesser say in the matter depend on the extent to which it can attract votes from other parties, including those who will be partners in a future coalition government.

This means that even those parties which will be partners in parliament are conditioned in the constituencies to think and act only as rivals. Partnership, when it comes, is restricted to the cabinet, and to a lesser degree to the parliamentary lobbies. It may be argued that the existence in 1919 of the Bloc National, in 1924 of the Cartel and in 1936 of the Popular Front affords

13

sufficient evidence to show that this obstacle is not insuperable. If post-war conditions were comparable, the argument might be valid. But they are not. Moreover these coalitions were primarily electoral coalitions, rather than agreements on a specific programme, of parliamentary action. Even the Popular Front, which did have a programme, could not hold together to carry it out, except for a short time and at the cost of a great deal of internal friction.

In other words, one of the biggest obstacles to the formation of two broad-based coalitions is the nature of French party organization. In the 1956 Assembly, there were only two workable combinations—a predominantly right-wing coalition, dependent on socialist support or neutrality, and a predominantly left-wing coalition, dependent either on right-wing or communist support. With a permanent opposition of nearly 200 deputies any government was obliged, in order to obtain a majority in the Assembly, to take into the coalition elements too far to the Right—or to the Left—to satisfy the bulk of its supporters. In these circumstances, a coalition easily breaks up. French right-wing parties do not constitute organized and disciplined formations. They have never been able to prevent individuals and small groups from breaking away and there is, therefore, every reason to think that a coalition relying on their support would not be much more stable than the present system.

But the greatest obstacle to the formation of two broad-based coalitions is the abnormality of the circumstances in which parliamentary government is called upon to function in France today. The bulk of the opposition to any government is an opposition, not so much to its policy as to its political philosophy. As Frenchmen so often put it, the crisis is not one of majorities; it is a crisis of the régime. The consequence is that democratic parties are compelled to work together, although their differences on policy may be greater than those that normally separate the British government and the opposition. As M. Goguel has shown, all that really unites the members of governmental coalitions in France is their common acceptance of democratic principles and the democratic methods of parliamentary government. However essential that unity may be, it is not enough to govern with.

Yet, in spite of all these economic and political obstacles, post-war France had in fact a surprising number of achievements to her credit. The economic revolution did, in fact go on after M. Mendès-France's defeat, with less spectacular publicity, under the premiership of his successor, and its effects became fully visible in 1955 and 1956. Stabilization of prices in 1952 and 1953 was followed by a period of steadily rising production, rising wages and by years of industrial peace and prosperity. The results of the first and second Monnet plans were seen in increased electrification, in the record production of cars, in improved agricultural production, in increased building construction. From 80,000 housing units in 1952, building construction rose to over 230,000 per annum, from 1956 onwards, a high proportion being provision for working class needs.

It is true that in 1957 France was once again confronting a serious economic crisis. But this was due in part to temporary factors—the frosts in the spring of 1956, and the cost of the Suez expedition in the autumn, in part to the inflationary effects of the expansion itself, and in part to the economic consequences of the Algerian war. Better paid workers were buying food, refrigerators, washing machines and cars that, in the interests of a sound economy, should have been diverted to the export market; particularly, when the maintenance in the forces of thousands of young men sent to Algeria was sending up the cost of labour, diverting raw materials from production for export, and threatening to slow down economic modernization.

By 1958, it was clear that, once again, both the economic and the political systems were being called upon to stand too great a strain. For a politician like M. Mendès-France, who was also an economist, the lesson was clear. It was the lesson of 1953. France must choose. She must either make peace in Algeria, or put her economy on a war footing. But French traditions, the intractable nature of the Algerian problem, and political divisions, on this and other questions, combined to make the choice impossible.

CHAPTER IX

FOREIGN PROBLEMS

IF France's post-war economic weakness was due in large part to the multiplicity of the demands that she was called on to meet, her weakness in the field of foreign affairs was, in the view of many British observers, attributable rather to the single-mindedness with which, after the war, she pursued the one predominant objective of making France safe from Germany. Even after the sovietization of the satellite countries, the tension of the months of the Berlin air-lift and the outbreak of the war in Korea, the majority of Frenchmen seemed to be far less conscious of the Russian than of the German danger.

The failure to achieve security. Nevertheless, the picture of French post-war foreign policy is complex, for several reasons. France's apparent obsession with Germany, sometimes to the exclusion of other issues, resulted in her being progressively out of step with her allies. The French political parties agreed neither on what would be the ideal solution, nor on what was the least unsatisfactory compromise possible in the circumstances. And when, after the outbreak of the war in Korea, the Americans decided, and the British reluctantly agreed, that German contingents would be necessary for the effective defence of Western Europe, there were disagreements within and between the French parties, regarding both the necessity for German rearmament and the conditions in which it could be achieved without danger to France.

To many Frenchmen, post-war foreign policy seems, in retrospect, to have consisted of a series of rearguard actions, in which France was compelled to renounce, one after the other, conditions which she had postulated as being essential to her security. In 1945 and 1946, France was insisting, as a minimum, on four safeguards; she wanted to prevent the creation of a German central government or at least to ensure that a future German state would not include the Rhineland, which ought, in her view, to be a separate state, subject to a prolonged period of allied military occupation; she wanted the Ruhr to be separated from Germany and to be placed under international control—a kind of allied trusteeship; she wanted the Saar to be administered as an autonomous territory and claimed the right to control its economic resources, in particular the mines, whose coal was needed for the Lorraine steel works; and finally, she wanted German industrial production to be restricted to a level low enough to ensure that Germany would not again be able to threaten the security of her neighbours.

By the end of 1946, the administrative and financial burden of occupation in the American and British zones had convinced both Anglo-Saxon governments that the industrial level would have to be raised if Germany were to be enabled to export enough to keep herself. With the economic fusion of the British and American zones in 1947 and of all three western zones in 1948, the creation of German central government departments became a necessary measure of economic co-ordination. By 1948, the failure to reach any agreement at the six meetings of Foreign Ministers which had been held since the end of the war, and the events leading up to the Berlin air-lift, had convinced both British and American governments that the creation of a West German state, including both the Ruhr and the Rhineland, was by now inevitable. The creation of central organs of government in the eastern zone made it also politically imperative for the western allies to organize the co-operation of their zones with the West, which meant recognizing some form of German government. In 1949, an Occupation Statute was signed and a German Federal constitution drawn up; before the end of the year, general elections had been held throughout the three western zones and the Federal Republic's first government had been formed under the direction of Dr. Adenauer.

France obtained partial satisfaction on two points only. The Saar remained an autonomous territory, whose economy was closely linked with that of France, and the Ruhr industries were placed under international supervision.

The Saar and the Ruhr. In 1947, France formed a customs and currency union with the Saar, a Saar constitution was accepted by a plebiscite and, as a result of general elections, a Saar government was set up under the leadership of the majority party, the Christian democrats. The constitution provided for economic union with France, but for political autonomy, except in the fields of defence and foreign relations. The Saar, that is, retained the German language and its traditional way of life and, from 1950, was separately represented (as an associate member) in the Council of Europe. But in the European economic bodies, such as O.E.E.C. and, from 1952 onwards, in the Coal and Steel Pool, the Saar continued to be represented by

France. A series of conventions signed in 1950 provided for administration of the Saar mines for fifty years by a joint board. The high officials were in the main French, however, and the real casting vote remained that of the French government. The Saar railways were also run by a joint board.

On the whole, this arrangement suited the political leaders of both France and the Saar. There were complaints on points of detail—regarding the Warndt mines, for example, or the share of Marshall Aid which has gone to equip the Saar mines. Claims by the Saar to greater autonomy in foreign affairs were met in 1952 by the promotion of the High Commissioner, M. Grandval, to the rank of Ambassador, and, in 1953, by the revision of the conventions in order to give the Saar a greater degree of autonomy.[1] But as Germany recovered her strength and prestige, her resentment at the political separation of the Saar increased. Matters came to a head in 1952 when elections were held in the Saar. They resulted in a large majority for the Christian democrats who were in favour of Saar autonomy, or of a not clearly defined 'European' status.[2] Germany was very dissatisfied with the position. She objected to the suppression of those political parties which had been carrying out violent pro-German propaganda. This had led, in the German view, to election results not reflecting accurately the real state of public opinion. She also objected strongly to any change in the status of the Saar—such as 'Europeanization'—which might appear

[1] The revised conventions were ratified by the French parliament in November 1953.
[2] The Saar was ready, said its Prime Minister in April 1951, 'to become a stone in the edifice of a united and pacific Europe'. In August 1950, Saarbrucken University expressed the wish to become the first 'European' university.

to envisage the permanent separation of the Saar from Germany, arguing that only the peace settlement could determine the permanent status of the Saar.

Franco-German disagreements regarding the Saar were again very much to the fore in 1953 when elections were held in Germany, for the closeness of the contest between German social democrats and Christian democrats led both to exploit the popular nationalist claim that the Saar was German. Although prepared for modifications of the Franco-Saar conventions on points of detail, France remained firmly determined to retain the present status, unless agreement could be reached on 'Europeanization'. Two new factors had, indeed, made this imperative from the French point of view. First, with the coming into force of the Schuman Plan, the Ruhr authority had ceased to exist. France's sole remaining safeguard of the original four which she had claimed in 1945 and 1946 was, therefore, her control of the economic resources of the Saar. She needed this control all the more now since, without it, she could be outvoted by Germany within the Coal-Steel Community. Second, she was by then apprehensive regarding her position *vis-à-vis* Germany, if the projected European Defence Community were to come into being and so was even less willing to give up her hold on the last remaining reinforcement against a, by now, economically strong and apparently politically stable Germany.

From 1952 to 1955, therefore, the question of the future of the Saar became inextricably involved in the general problem of Franco-German relations and the place of Germany in Western Europe.

France's European policy. From 1949 onwards, the failure of the allies to agree and the emergence of a German state had led France to seek further safeguards against any possibility of a renewed threat of German aggression within the framework of a united Europe. France's 'European' policy went through three stages. At first, she hoped for some form of political integration —loosely referred to as federation. But Great Britain and the Scandinavian countries refused to follow her along this road, preferring the traditional method of governmental co-operation, either direct, or through existing organizations such as O.E.E.C. From 1950 onwards, therefore, France turned to the idea of functional integration and took the lead in the movement for its achievement. It had been hoped that the Schuman Plan, proposed by France in May 1950 and intended to be the first of a series of experiments in functional co-ordination,[1] would prove acceptable to Great Britain. But the British held aloof for two principal reasons. First, they disliked being tied down by precise written commitments at the beginning of a new venture which seemed to them to call for practical experiment, based on the method of trial and error. Second, they were not prepared to commit themselves to abandon sovereignty within the field of the experiment to a 'supra-national' authority. The six countries, therefore, went ahead, counting on Great Britain's benevolent 'association'—a term whose implications were never clearly defined— and hoping that at a later stage Great Britain would be

[1] Special committees were set up to prepare draft proposals for similar authorities to deal with European Transport and Agriculture, but by the end of 1953 neither project had advanced beyond the preparatory stage. The only European authority in process of creation was the European Defence Community (see below, pp. 195–202). An *ad hoc* committee of the Consultative Assembly had agreed on draft proposals for a European political authority 'with limited functions but real powers' but these had not been accepted by the national governments of the six countries.

prepared to co-operate more fully with them. The Schuman Plan Treaty was signed in Paris in April 1951 and was ratified by all six member countries.[1] The institutions provided for in the Treaty were set up in 1952. The first stages of the application of the plan date from July of that year and it entered fully into operation a year later, at which date the Ruhr authority ceased to exist.

The problem of German rearmament. Up to the outbreak of the war in Korea, there had been no question of any German participation in either European or Atlantic defence. In July 1949, M. Schuman had stated that, 'Germany has no army and must not have one'. But in September 1950, America submitted a plan for a German defence contribution and Great Britain reluctantly agreed in principle to the formation of German contingents. The French government, torn between its dislike of any form of German rearmament and its fear that a refusal to agree to it would only lead to direct negotiations between the United States and Germany, which might lead in turn to the revival of the *Wehrmacht* and a German General Staff, accepted reluctantly what seemed the lesser evil, namely, the incorporation of German contingents in a European army. And so France's European policy entered on a third stage. To the Schuman Plan there was added in October 1950 the Pleven Plan for a European army. From then, up to the end of 1953, France once again fought what looked to her a series of rearguard actions as, one by one, the various safeguards proposed by her were rejected by the Germans or by Great Britain or the United States. France's position was, by then, of course, relatively weaker because she now had to reckon with a Germany

[1] The French ratified in April 1953.

conscious of her value to Western defence and prepared to drive a hard bargain for every concession.

To begin with, the project for a European army raised a number of problems, on which either Germany, or the allies, or the French parties themselves were not agreed. The French insisted at first that all units larger than 800–1,200 men should be 'integrated', that is, should be of mixed nationalities. Their aim was to provide German soldiers, without incurring the risk of re-creating a German army and a German General Staff. This solution was not acceptable to France's partners in European defence, mainly for technical reasons. The Germans were prepared to contribute only on certain conditions, among which were agreement on the problem of the Saar and complete equality, which, as was made clear at the beginning of 1952, was interpreted to mean the right to membership of N.A.T.O. Since N.A.T.O. is an alliance of national armies, this was obviously unacceptable to the French. But the French were far from being agreed among themselves on the form which the German contribution to European defence ought to take. The communists were, of course, opposed to the whole idea of German rearmament. But some non-communist opinion—in particular some members of the socialist party—although in favour of a European army, argued against the inclusion in it of German contingents. They held that it was not safe to rearm Germans so soon after the war, and while the newly created democratic institutions of the Federal Republic were not firmly established. The Germans were undeniably nationalist and many of them were openly claiming as a right the restitution of their pre-war frontiers. The obvious objection to leaving the Germans unarmed, namely, that this placed France at a great economic disadvantage, burdened as she was both by her contribution to European defence and her long war in Indo-China, was only half-met by the suggestion that Germany should be asked for an industrial, instead of a military contribution. Nor was there at any stage evidence that such a solution would be acceptable either to the United States or to Germany itself.

At the other political extreme, the Gaullists did not object to German rearmament but had little or no faith in the proposed European army as a defence against German aggressiveness. They preferred an old-style Franco-German alliance (provided France retained the lead in Europe) to new-fangled and ill-defined plans for integration which, in the words of one of them, sought 'to transform the Germans into compatriots in order to avoid having them for allies',[1] and which risked compromising the future of the French army, without, in their view, providing any effective guarantees against the revival of a German army.

From the European Army to the European Defence Community. In between these two extremes, the governmental parties and the majority of the socialists supported the idea of a European army, but with very differing emphases. Some were enthusiastic, seeing in the European army a new and hopeful development towards an international order; others supported the idea reluctantly, because they saw no other way of avoiding worse evils. They counted on the existence of a European army to prevent the Americans from pressing for the re-creation of a German national army or from threatening to give up the attempt to defend Europe. They counted on German integration in Western Europe to prevent

[1] Robert Aron in *Le Problème allemand* (La Nef-Julliard, 1952), p. 8.

the Germans from trying to play off the East against the West or from getting industrially too far ahead of the French. They were conscious, however, that a rearmed Germany would constitute a potential danger and so included in the project a number of conditions designed to make German rearmament safe for Europe. Unfortunately, among the conditions were provisions for a 'supra-national' European authority and for the participation, or at least 'association', of Great Britain. Great Britain officially agreed to 'association', but not in the sense in which most Frenchmen understood it.

That was the general situation when, in February 1952, the project for a European Defence Community was debated in the French Assembly. The Assembly finally approved the text of the resolution, which the government had made a question of confidence, by 327 votes to 287. A detailed examination of the figures reveals, however, that all the parties, with the exception of the communists and the Gaullists, were divided. Moreover, the resolution itself contained a number of ambiguities and the socialist vote (without which the government would not have obtained a majority at all) was accompanied by a number of conditions—or mental reservations—on precisely those points on which the allies were known not to share the French viewpoint. Thus, the resolution stated specifically that Germany's inclusion in the European army did not imply that she would be admitted to membership of N.A.T.O., a point which the Germans had conceded with great unwillingness, and purely as a temporary measure; it called for integration 'at the lowest possible level', without specifying what that implied, although the debate had revealed the serious disquiet of some deputies at France's acceptance of German units much larger than those originally proposed; it asked that everything should be done to ensure the subordination of the European army to 'a supra-national political authority, with limited but real powers, responsible to the representatives of the parliaments or the peoples of Europe', a requirement which, if met, would, as all Frenchmen were by then fully aware, rule out British participation of the kind appealed for in the final paragraph of the resolution, and regarded by many Frenchmen as the only satisfactory form of British guarantee.

The ambiguities had not been cleared up when France and Germany signed the Treaty in May 1952, nor were they cleared up during the next two years. Meanwhile, a number of new difficulties had cropped up. First, it had been agreed at the Lisbon meeting of Foreign Ministers which took place immediately after the Assembly's vote, that no German contingents should be formed until the Treaty had been ratified. It was ratified by Germany in March 1953, but, as a result of disagreements within all parties in France (except the communists), and of disagreements between France and Germany, French ratification was continually delayed, and, on 30 August 1954, finally refused.

There were three principal reasons for France's hesitations. First, in March 1952, had come the Soviet note to the three Western governments proposing a four-power conference with a view to determining the conditions in which German unification could be brought about, and a German government representing the whole of Germany enabled to participate in the drawing up of a peace treaty. The second reason for hesitation was the continued failure of Great Britain and France to agree on a definition of 'association' which sufficiently reassured the French. And the third was the failure of

France and Germany to settle the outstanding problem of the Saar. Both regarded a settlement as an essential condition of German rearmament. But each laid down conditions that were unacceptable to the other.

The Russian proposal was particularly welcome to those sections of opinion in France which had opposed German rearmament all along, namely, the socialist minority already referred to, and the less easily defined sections of opinion generally described as 'neutralist', who had opposed both the creation of a European army and French membership of the Atlantic Pact. To these Frenchmen, the Soviet offer provided a pretext for putting off German rearmament at least until the possibilities of reaching some understanding with the Soviet Union had been further explored. To the German socialist party it provided an argument for putting it off until the possibility of Russian agreement to German unification had been explored.

The first effect of the Russian note was thus to intensify French divisions, because other Frenchmen, while no less convinced of the need to seek an understanding with Russia, were equally convinced that France ought not to interrupt her programme of European integration in order to do so. They feared, indeed, that that might perhaps be precisely what the Russian note was intended to achieve. It was argued on the one hand that to pursue the policy of making the Federal Republic an integral part of the West European group was to prejudice any chance there might be of persuading Russia to agree either to German unification or to some mitigation of the cold war; it was argued on the other hand that if such a chance did in reality now exist, it was in all probability a consequence of the growing strength of the West, and that if that were so, while something might be gained if the West were to negotiate from strength, nothing would be gained if the West were to abandon its most powerful bargaining weapon before the negotiations began.

From European deadlock to Common Market. By the end of 1953, France's European policy had reached a threefold deadlock. There seemed no means by which agreement could be reached, either between France and Germany, or between France and Great Britain, on the points which were responsible for French reluctance to ratify the European Defence Community Treaty. In the absence of such an agreement, French ratification seemed unlikely. Yet no alternative policy could command a majority in the Assembly.

The French tended to blame the British for the deadlock, since the main cause of French dissatisfaction with the Treaty was the British decision to remain aloof. The policy of European integration, so enthusiastically adopted by Frenchmen in 1949, had always been based on the assumption that Great Britain would be a partner, whose power and prestige would enable France to prevent German domination in Europe. The British tended to blame the French for the deadlock, first on the ground that they had, from the outset, postulated as a condition of European functional co-operation in the Schuman Plan and the European army the 'supranational' principle, and second for their apriorist methods. In the British view, both these approaches were known to the French to be unacceptable to the British.

Whatever the causes of the deadlock, and wherever the real responsibility lay, the principal consequences of Anglo-French disagreement were first, that, three years after M. Pleven had put forward his proposal, the existence of a European army, even on paper, was still

14

in doubt and Germany was, therefore, still contributing no manpower to European defence;[1] and second, that France, as a member of 'little Europe' was confronting precisely the danger that she had been so strenuously seeking to guard against, namely, the danger of German domination in Europe.

In the circumstances it was remarkable that, once ratification of E.D.C. had been refused by France, Franco-German relations should so quickly have been improved and further steps towards European integration contemplated. Three things, in particular, made this rapid progress possible. The first was the new British commitment in Europe under the Paris Treaties voted by the Assembly in October 1954. Suggestions for an extension of the membership and functions of the Brussels Treaty Organization were regarded in France as hopeful starting-points for the evolution of a Europe in which Great Britain would be a full partner. And though these hopes were not realized in the following years, they did serve, in 1954, to sugar the pill of German re-armament and German membership of N.A.T.O., sufficiently to persuade the French Parliament to accept them. The second contribution to the improvement of Franco-German relations was the settlement of the problem of the Saar. On 23 October 1955 a referendum was held on the Saar Statute, provided for in the Franco-German Agreement which formed part of the Paris Treaties. Saarlanders rejected the Statute by a large majority. From then onwards, French opinion became resigned to the inevitability of the return of the Saar to Germany. A series of agreements governing the incorporation of the

[1] A four Power agreement of 26 February 1952 laid down the amount of the financial contribution to be made by Germany to European defence.

Saar in the West German Federal Republic were signed in October 1956. From the beginning of 1957, the Saar became politically a part of Germany. Her economic integration was not to be completed for three years.

The third factor making possible Franco-German co-operation was the coincidence that for sixteen months during this vital period (from February 1956 to May 1957) both France and Germany had governments headed by ardent believers in the policy of European integration. With the apparent settlement of the two outstanding Franco-German differences, namely, those concerning German rearmament and the future of the Saar, the European movement regained some of its impetus, encouraged by Dr. Adenauer and M. Guy Mollet. Though a French plan, put forward at the beginning of 1955, for the creation of a European Arms Pool with a supra-national authority came to nothing, European co-operation in the atomic field was achieved with the voting of the Rome Treaties on 24 March 1957, Treaties which also provided for the setting-up, as from the beginning of 1958, of a Common Market between France, Italy, Germany and Benelux. That section of French opinion (of which M. Guy Mollet is a leader) which still hoped eventually for European political integration saw in the Common Market the beginnings of a new development that might provide a surer route towards a politically unified Europe than the elaboration of a European constitution, which the six nations had attempted, and failed to agree on, in 1953.

Some sections of French opinion were sceptical, though for different reasons. A number of difficult technical problems had still to be resolved before the Common Market could become a reality and, by the autumn of 1957, France's economic difficulties were creating doubts in some quarters regarding her ability to compete on equal terms with Germany.

France and the World. Unfortunately for France, the apparent settlement of the German problem was accompanied by a worsening of her relations with the two North African Protectorates. By 1951, relations with both Tunisia and Morocco had reached a state of deadlock. The ending of the eight-year war in Indo-China, with the Geneva Settlement of July 1954, in one sense eased French problems, since it removed a heavy military burden that had contributed to France's sense of inferiority in Europe. In another, however, it added to her problems. The lessening of American aid produced a dollar shortage, and the fact that the Geneva Settlement meant the loss of Indo-China, once the immediate shock of the French defeat at Dien-Bien-Phu (which M. Mendès-France used successfully to try to break the Tunisian deadlock) had worn off, produced a climate which intensified the resistance of the centre and right-wing parties to any suggestion of Algerian independence, even at some future date, as constituting a policy of 'abandon' in North Africa.

Under the impetus of M. Mendès-France's dynamic premiership, negotiations for the grant of home rule to Tunisia were begun in September 1954. Terrorism, which had been a problem for several years, ceased almost overnight, in response to a joint appeal by French and Tunisian governments. And, though the negotiations proved difficult, an agreement was signed in June 1955, providing for home rule, France remaining responsible only for defence and security, and for police control in so far as it was necessary during the period of the gradual transfer of responsibilities to Tunisia.

Talks were begun with Moroccan representatives in

1955 and an agreement was reached in November. The former Sultan, whose nationalist sympathies had led in 1953 to his deposition and exile by the French, returned to Rabat, undertaking to set up a constitutional government and to negotiate with France the conditions of Moroccan independence.

In fact, Tunisian and Moroccan nationalism set a pace that led to complete *de facto* independence more speedily than France had intended. On 2 March 1956 Morocco's independence was formally recognized, including her right to possess a national army and to control her own foreign policy. The recognition of Tunisia's independence on similar terms followed on 20 March. But neither Franco-Tunisian, nor Franco-Moroccan negotiations led to any agreement on the 'interdependence', which France had regarded as a necessary corollary to the grant of home rule.

There was, indeed, a continuous state of friction, first regarding the status of French troops in both countries and, second, as a consequence of the spread of the Algerian rebellion, regarding the rights of Algeria to independence. Both Morocco and Tunisia supported the claims of the rebels and there were frequent frontier incidents. The situation on the Algerio-Tunisian frontier became serious at the beginning of 1958, when, after a number of incidents, both France and Tunisia took their complaints to the United Nations. France maintained that Tunisia was providing not only a rebel base, but also a steady supply of arms, and a section of opinion in France had begun, by then, to feel that, if it were not for outside help from neighbouring Arab States, the Algerian rebellion would already have been subdued. Tunisia complained of frontier violations by France and demanded the withdrawal of all French troops from

Tunisia, including Bizerta, equipped by the French to serve as an essential part of North African defence. The consequences of all this were that France felt herself increasingly isolated and doubly weakened. First, she felt keenly her loss of prestige as a Great Power, both *vis-à-vis* the West and the Arab world, owing to the loss of her far-Eastern and North African possessions and the threatened loss of Algeria. Both Tunisian and Moroccan governments reiterated their desire to remain on good terms with France. Both countries sought (and obtained) economic aid from France. Yet while the Algerian problem remained unsolved, no progress could be made towards the development of a stable Franco-North African community.

Secondly, France felt weakened in her relations with the rest of the world. She resented criticisms by her allies of her North African policy even though they did not challenge her juridical right to regard Africa as a domestic matter. She insisted on her rights under the United Nations Charter to regard intervention, either by the United Nations Assembly or by any country, as unjustifiable. Much diplomatic effort was concentrated, from 1955 to 1957, on preventing a vote in the United Nations Assembly hostile to French policy in Algeria. The Suez expedition, in November 1956, was regarded by the majority of Frenchmen more as an essential step towards the solution of the Algerian problem than as a reaction against Colonel Nasser's unilateral repudiation of an international agreement, and French public opinion, on the Left as well as on the Right, was far more whole-heartedly in support of the Suez intervention than was British opinion. The decision by the British and American Governments to send a small consignment of arms to Tunisia on 15 November 1957 was the occasion of an outburst of anti-British feeling, unequalled since the war.

In other words, the inferiority complex from which France has suffered since the war in the field of foreign affairs, instead of disappearing with the settlement of the German problem, found a fresh stimulus in France's failure to solve the Algerian problem.

CHAPTER X

THE MIND OF POST-WAR FRANCE

The post-war psychological malaise. It has been one of
the contentions of the preceding chapters that 'two
things are wrong with France: the accumulated burdens
of war and the non-existence of effective government',[1]
and that these two problems have so reacted on each
other as to render both intractable. It has sometimes
seemed to France's neighbours and allies that the intractability might be more apparent than real and that
the persistence of political deadlock might be due to a
lack of the will rather than of the power to end it. British
critics have tended to become exasperated by French
party divisions and by the readiness of the parties to
overthrow governments; 'France's petty politics stop
policy making.'[2] Or they see in French negativism and
'insularity' symptoms of a deep-seated psychological
maladjustment.

'The low morale of the French,' wrote a commenta-
tor in 1950, 'their lack of confidence in their own
statesmen and that brilliant scepticism which they
confuse with political realism, together lead some of
them to nag a good friend and to disparage the many
real concessions that have been made to their point of
view.

'There are two other characteristics of French post-

[1] *Observer,* 9.3.52.   [2] *Economist,* 24.3.51.

war attitudes which may baffle but should not be allowed to irritate their British friends. First, is the educated Frenchman's habit of presenting a political or economic dilemma with the pride and delight that his wife shows in offering a well-chosen meal. The second is his reluctance to recognize any logic but his own. He seems only too anxious to show the unpredictability of human affairs and the futility of making any strenuous effort to control them.'[1]

British criticisms of this kind have certainly both baffled and irritated the French, who have felt that, where nagging was concerned, they were the injured party. Frenchmen who recognize their own low morale, their lack of confidence, negativism, or even 'insularity', would nevertheless argue that these are symptoms rather than causes and that much of the responsibility for them is attributable to Great Britain, without whose 'negative' approach to France's European policy, inspired by the 'insularity' of her Commonwealth preoccupations, France would not have remained up to 1954 in an impasse, torn between the twin evils of E.D.C. and German membership of N.A.T.O.

It remains a fact, however, that, in spite of their resentment at times at the tone of British or American criticism, the French have been, since the war, their own most severe critics. Statesmen as far apart politically as M. Paul Reynaud and M. Mendès-France have agreed in much of their analysis of the inadequacy of French economic policy. M. Reynaud even went so far as to describe France in 1953 as 'the sick man of Europe'.[2] The negativism of the French Assembly has been frequently criticized by deputies themselves and a

[1] Ibid., 2.3.50.   [2] Investiture speech of 27.5.53.

number of proposals have been put forward to remedy it. As far back as 1952, one of the chief supporters of the government's 1958 constitutional amendments bill, which includes provisions designed to do this, drew the attention of his colleagues to the urgent need for action.

'This common front of refusal,' he said, 'is driving the country to irreparable disaster in both internal and external affairs. Standards of behaviour, both of public bodies and of individuals, have declined to an alarmingly low level. At the beginning of this parliament, when the problem could easily have been dealt with, the Assembly refused to pay any attention to it. Now it is high time for men of all parties, who are clear-sighted enough to realize the seriousness of the situation, to make up their minds to find a remedy for it.'[1]

M. Herriot, when President of the Assembly, and M. Auriol, when President of the Republic, frequently deplored the behaviour of deputies, the latter even going so far as to speak of 'a moral and spiritual crisis' during the five-week search for a government in June 1953. Statesmen, publicists and political scientists have drawn attention to the dangers of political instability, of anarchic parliamentary habits, to the persistence of pro-Communist obsessions.

These, and many other condemnations of French management of affairs since the war, reveal clearly the existence of a serious dissatisfaction, even more acutely felt by politically aware Frenchmen than by foreigners. The seven and a half million citizens who, in January 1956, voted either for the Poujadists or the Communists,

[1] M. Lecourt (MRP) in the Assembly, on 13.12.52.

though they were directly contributing to the perpetuation of parliamentary negativism, bear witness to the extent to which the average citizen, too, is critical of the parties that have governed France since the war and is looking elsewhere for France's salvation. Foreign visitors to France have noted the widening gulf between the elector and his representatives, the extent to which the French citizen has lost, or is losing, his interest in politics as well as his faith in politicians. They have noted, for example, the apathy, or cynicism, which has replaced impatience when governments fall; the passivity, or resignation, with which the French public put up with the inconvenience of strikes in essential public services or in national theatres. Both inside and outside France there have been comments on public ignorance of economic realities,[1] on public indifference to international issues, and particularly to the European problems which have so impassioned and embittered party relations in the National Assembly.

In September 1953, M. Mendès-France warned his compatriots that they were living in 1788.[2] The comment of a number of them was that, if the situation in 1953 was pre-revolutionary, the revolutionaries were conspicuous by their absence. In 1958, in spite of the economic crisis of the previous autumn, the general economic situation was much better than it had been in 1953. Yet the political situation was in many respects worse.

If it were necessary to sum up in one word the predominant mood of post-war France from 1946 onwards that word would be 'disillusionment'. No doubt much

[1] See, for example, the essay by M. Mendès-France in *Le franc, mythe et réalité* (La Nef-Julliard, 1953), p. 239.
[2] Speech made on 20 September 1953 at the radical party congress at Aix-les-Bains.

of this disillusionment can still be accounted for by the exhaustion of the war years and the effort of reconstruction. No doubt, too, some of the exhilaration of the immediate post-war period—the revolutionary idealism that inspired both the economic and social reforms of the provisional governments and the decision to give France a new constitution—was a natural reaction to liberation, rather than a positive philosophy, just as some of the later depression was a natural reaction to the psychological and material difficulties of the post-war years, rather than a fundamental pessimism. There is more to it than that, however. There is an intellectual and psychological *malaise* in France which is of long standing. The strain of the post-war years helped to deepen it, but its roots were there before the war.

Insecurity and the sense of defeat. First and foremost, France emerged from the Second World War, technically on the side of the victors, but in reality with a deep-seated sense of defeat, which the disappointments of post-war foreign policy gradually transformed into a pessimism, or defeatism, deepened by pre-war memories. The long struggle for security in the pre-war years had created a wide-spread feeling of helplessness in the face of an inexorable threat, before Munich added its quota of humiliation. The 'lost generation' of the First World War had meant shortage of manpower, both of skilled labour and political leadership. Economic progress had been retarded and production and productivity were both lower in 1939 than they had been ten years earlier. Political stability had been undermined by the growth of anti-democratic forces. Military efficiency had been sacrificed to a mirage—the conception of static defence embodied in the Maginot Line. France was economically, politically and militarily unprepared for war, and partly, though not entirely, for those reasons, was also psychologically unprepared. She was suffering from war-weariness before war broke out. Both on the Right and on the non-communist Left, there were strong movements in favour of appeasement. Among left-wing intellectuals, and particularly in the teaching profession, pacifism was strong.

Many non-pacifists, however, had watched the approach of war with a sense of paralysed helplessness, caused not merely by their own unreadiness, but by the unreadiness and the unawareness of danger of their British allies, who, in the spring of 1939, had still not felt war to be imminent enough to warrant the introduction of conscription.

This mood was eloquently expressed by Georges Duhamel, in a collection of essays published just before war broke out.[1] In one of them, he recalls a visit to England in the spring, and the sense, which British failure to recognize the nearness of war gave him, of being a death's head at the feast.

'A Frenchman', he wrote, 'hangs his head and thinks, though does not say so aloud, that in this world, the gift of imagination has been very unevenly divided. . . . He reflects with anguish that all triumphant civilizations have created a grace and harmony such as is found here and have abhorred disorder and bloodshed, but that the day has come when the Barbarian has reappeared and the task has had to be begun all over again. Two years ago, I brought with me from Paris a bunch of lilies of the valley and it was still fresh when I reached Victoria.

[1] *Mémorial de la Guerre Blanche* (Mercure de France, 1939), p. 113.

"Next time," I said to my friends, "since the journey is so short, I shall bring you a soap bubble."

'I brought no soap bubble with me. I brought only my sadness and my anxiety. Once again, I walked through the gardens full of flowers and watched lovely young mothers playing with their children. I thought with pain as I contemplated this happy race: "They believe the fire to be so far away. Its scorching heat does not touch them." Alas! when the first of these young English mothers utters her first cry of despair, I think that I shall hear it from Paris.'

This was the mood of many thinking Frenchmen when war came in 1939. When it had been won, they set out once again to make France safe from invasion and war. This time, Germany must be kept weak; this time Europe must combine to restrain Germain aggressiveness. Gradually, as the hopes of keeping Germany weak faded, and as the first plans for European integration had to be watered down in the face of British and Scandinavian disagreements with the French approach, Frenchmen, recalling the recovery of Germany in the thirties and the failure of France and Great Britain to keep in step, began to say, with despair: 'We have been here before.'

The obstacles to Franco-British understanding and co-operation have already been analysed. What France's allies, and Great Britain in particular, have sometimes failed to allow for is the strength of the French feeling of standing by, helplessly watching history repeat itself, and the consequent sense of despair and defeat which lay behind 'neutralist' escapism, and perhaps also behind the no less escapist unreality of the grandiloquent claims of right-wing and Gaullist opinion to European leadership.

Conservatism and the sense of frustration. The second cause of post-war disillusionment came from the perpetuation of pre-war political divisions and the consequent impression created in the mind of the average citizen that the politicians were fiddling while Rome burned, or playing for their own hand, or merely behaving irresponsibly.

'Our misfortune in France', wrote M. Beuve-Méry, 'is that governments no longer choose. They depend on narrow and unstable majorities, they are short-sighted and uncertain. Inevitably, they are obsessed by the need for self-preservation and so tend to come down on the side that will involve the fewest difficulties for them in the immediate future. They no longer solve problems, they put off the evil day, and when they can no longer do that, they accept the inevitable.'[1]

'We do not take governmental crises seriously,' wrote M. Rémy Roure in January 1952. 'This is merely the seventeenth in seven years! But we ought to take them seriously, very seriously.'[2]

The failure of both politicians and public to treat political crises with the seriousness that the circumstances demanded, or with the seriousness with which they have been treated by France's neighbours and allies, is a result neither of original sin nor of frivolity, but is, in large part, the result of a pressure of events which drove opinion back to pre-war modes of thought. The conservatism of French social and economic life has been recognized by students of French civilization for generations. But political conservatism is something

---

[1] *Réflexions Politiques, 1932–52* (Paris, Editions du Seuil, 1952), pp. 233–4.
[2] *Le Monde*, 9.1.52.

that, up to the twentieth century, France has rarely been accused of. Indeed, it has been a commonplace that, while Great Britain's individualism has tended to express itself in moral terms—in the proliferation of dissident sects and odd religions—French individualism has been mainly political, and the history of French political ideas can provide examples of almost every conceivable kind of Utopia, from Rousseau's Social Contract to Fourier's *phalanges*, and of almost every type of political organization, from Proudhon's syndicalism and Saint-Simon's pseudo-scientific technocracy to the Marxism and social-democracy of twentieth-century political thinkers.

Why has this ferment of revolutionary thought given way to largely backward-looking political attitudes? The answer lies, partly in the nature of the modern challenge to political thinkers, partly in the absence in France of the external aids to adaptation that Great Britain was able to profit from.

All European countries emerged from the war impoverished and faced with the need to adapt themselves to the changed economic, political, and international circumstances of the post-war world. In Great Britain, a number of factors facilitated these adaptations. The need to make industry more efficient and to expand exports had been driven home to numbers of British citizens in the thirties by the existence of over a million unemployed. There was a general recognition of the need for continued governmental direction in the immediate post-war years in order to enable Great Britain to recover her economic health. Party conflicts were, therefore, relatively free from bitterness and much of the mutual respect engendered by co-operation in war-time governments survived the ending of the political truce in 1945. The war-time apparatus of planned production and distribution provided ready-made administrative and technical machinery for the application of post-war controls. And the British citizen was, on the whole, psychologically prepared to accept 'austerity', partly out of fear of a return of unemployment, partly because rationing had worked well during the war and he had come to appreciate its advantages, partly, too, because the war-time recognition of Britain's strategic vulnerability had given him a psychological shake-up, which made him ready to abandon some aspects of his secular way of life.

France emerged from the war with both an administrative and a political machine that had to be reconstituted before they could begin to function properly, and with economic and fiscal systems that had been out-of-date for years before the war and were peculiarly unamenable to controls of any kind, let alone the drastic controls which post-war recovery required. Moreover, France's experience of war-time controls, whether imposed by Vichy or by the German authorities, had hardly been of a nature to encourage respect for controls in themselves, or for the state's agents who would have to apply them.

The psychological obstacles to adaptation in France were indeed overwhelming. The French had suffered far more than the British from real hunger and from shortages of consumer goods. The dislocation of family and economic life caused by the occupation and the absence in Germany of over two million prisoners and workers had created a passionate desire to get back to normal. And there had been nothing spectacular about the experience of the pre-war years—no wide-spread unemployment, for instance—to bring home to the

French citizen the need for radical changes in the familiar economic and social organization of society. All the pull, then, was towards the familiar, the normal, pre-war way of life. And getting back to normal meant a return to political as well as to economic conservatism. French politics had been in cold storage for four years. Old differences had been put aside, but not settled.

In an address given in America in 1950, M. André Siegfried spoke of the changes that the last two generations had brought to France, of the development of mechanization, the growth of inflation, the demoralization that was a natural concomitant of war.

'Last but not least,' he concluded, 'there is the shifting of the centre of gravity of the world, with the loss for Europe of her place at the head of world events. Taking all these grave circumstances into account, we can only ask ourselves: Will they prove stronger than the French tradition of twenty centuries? *Je me pose la question.*'[1]

His question was answered during the following years. Unfortunately for France, 'the French tradition of twenty centuries'—or at least of one century—proved stronger than the recognition that what the circumstances demanded was its radical adaptation. The result has been that, since the war, France has been out of step with the other nations of Europe, economically and to some extent politically, a pre-war survival in a post-war world. The need for internal economic reforms and the political obstacles to their achievement have been discussed in an earlier chapter. The need for economic adaptation in the international field was no less urgent.

[1] *Modern France* (Princeton, 1951), p. 16.

Even, in European affairs, France for long combined a traditional attachment to the formulation of general internationalist principles, and to theoretical, often oratorical, gestures, with a no less traditional attachment to economic nationalism, with the incongruous result that the leading spirit in the move towards European integration had the highest tariff barriers in Europe. M. André Siegfried has himself drawn attention to the French characteristic which can permit such a contradiction to persist. 'Strongly as a Frenchman may assert a principle,' he said, 'he remains unconvinced that the consequences of that principle should apply to him.'[1]

This conclusion really does less than justice to the French citizen. Over a century ago, Alexis de Tocqueville noted, among the many contradictions inherent in the French character, that of being able to combine extreme individualism with heroic patriotism; 'today the sworn foe of all obedience, tomorrow serving with a sort of passion'.[2] The war-time resistance movement provided ample confirmation, if any were needed, of the Frenchman's ability and readiness to use his individualism in the service of a national cause, and to sacrifice his life for it if the circumstances demanded that.

What, more than anything else, prevented the citizen from realizing the relation between principle and practice was the gulf between electors, party machines and governments. That gulf is due partly, as has been seen, to electoral habits which rob the elector of any direct sense of responsibility for what his representatives are doing. But it is, by now, difficult to decide exactly

---

[1] *Modern France* (Princeton, 1951), p. 14.
[2] Quoted in Soltau, R. H., *French Political Thought in the Nineteenth Century* (Benn, 1931), p. 494.

how far electoral habits represent a cause or an effect, because, in the absence of the political leadership that could have turned his attention to new problems, the elector has naturally clung to the familiar. When it fails to give him what he wants, or what he feels is his due, his tendency is not to try to change his political habits—the impetus for that must come from his political leaders— but to lose interest in politics altogether.

> '. . . the country is tired of politics but anxious for their results. It is this circumstance which makes the parties, with their tenaciously held verbal theories, obsolete. For the prime need now is for a common minimal national programme.'[1]

A national programme, however, is precisely what is ruled out by the political conservatism which is the consequence of the elector's frustration, and which now seems characteristic of deputies and electors alike. Events have their share of responsibility. Hard-pressed politicians, subject to attack from both Right and Left and harried from crisis to crisis, have had no time to stop and think out their political philosophies afresh. They have been unable to look farther ahead than the next confidence vote in the Assembly, or the next budget, or the next meeting of the United Nations Assembly and so have tended to fall back on familiar attitudes. And among these familiar attitudes there is that political conservatism (which France's neighbours call 'insular') that makes Frenchmen see modern problems in an intellectual framework appropriate to the past. The twentieth century is an age of techniques and expertise. Eighteenth-century universalism is of little use in dealing with the twentieth-century problems of the dollar gap

---

[1] *Economist*, 30.6.51.

and the European Payments Union. Yet, one of the permanent traits of French politics, as was noted at the beginning of this book, remains a lack of interest, on the part both of politicians and of the public, in the techniques of administration and the practical consequences of economic and political principles.

M. Siegfried accused his compatriots of not intending principles to be applied to themselves. The truth is rather that too many French citizens do not realize how and where the principles will or ought to affect them, because they are temperamentally uninterested in anything but the general principles, because they are bored by technical details and because there has been no serious effort by any section of the community to persuade them to change their habit of mind. Here the responsibility is primarily attributable to the political parties, which have failed in the task of educating public opinion in political and economic realities. And they have failed, partly because they have been too busy fighting old battles again, to devote enough time and energy to turning themselves into efficient instruments either of propaganda, or of government. They have lacked realistic policies, techniques of compromise, and (the Right and Radicals) methods of disciplining their members in the Assembly.

Fortunately for France, she has a number of scientists and technicians who *are* interested in techniques, who are among the best in the world and who possess in high degree the qualities of balanced and accurate judgement so often lacking in politicians. But owing to the discredit attaching to politics they have become infected with the complementary disease of disinterest in the general principles beloved by the politician. Too many of them have contracted out of politics. This divorce between the politician and the technician renders more complete the divorce between principles and practice. Conservatism and frustration have led to a situation in which, in everything but a still problematical 'Europeanism', the French citizen today, is in danger of being imprisoned in the past.

The spiritual vacuum and the sense of futility. The third, and perhaps the most profound, cause of postwar disillusionment is directly related to this political conservatism. Even if the French elector and his government were in close contact, if the electoral system were such that the elector felt that his vote gave him a real voice in the determination of government policy, he would still be left with the problem of deciding what to vote for. The 'minimal programme', which represents for the correspondent quoted above 'a prime need', does not yet exist. Since the war, the French citizen has, in the main, voted *against* something and in the National Assembly, deputies have come more and more to vote against policies instead of for them. For four years, French resisters fought the forces that threatened French survival as a nation. From 1947 to 1951, French citizens fought the forces, whether communist or Gaullist, that seemed to threaten democracy.

But what do Frenchmen want to fight *for*? The important fact about modern France is not the existence of political divisions. What matters is what the divisions are *about* and what political parties and the public feel that they should do about them. As long as the French citizen remains unsure on this point, his fundamental conservatism will lead him to resent changes. He must first be convinced that the sacrifices involved will be worth while.

The uncertainty, the despair and the sense of futility

created by this post-war political vacuum are nowhere more clearly seen than in post-war French literature. Existentialism, for instance, looked less like a philosophy than a symptom of nervous breakdown. Its emphasis on the concrete, on what exists, surely represented a reaction against the traditional rationalist approach, against the abstractions which are today no longer able to provide the answers to French problems. The conception of freedom as an expression of the individual will, divorced both from the limitations imposed by circumstances and from the social purpose imparted by an ideal, surely represented the reaction of an individualism which feels itself profoundly threatened both by national weakness and by the loss of a national purpose. The admission that 'each one of our acts sets in motion whatever gives meaning to the world and decides the place of man in the universe',[1] unaccompanied apparently by any sense of the need to combine such acts (or perhaps of the possibility of combining them) in order to give them social as well as individual meaning, surely argued a moral defeatism of which 'neutralism' was merely one facet. 'Existence,' says Sartre, 'is reasonless, causeless and unnecessary. We are born for no reason, go on living because we are weak and our death is decided by chance.'[2]

This form of negativism, which, with neutralism, has received more publicity outside France than any other of the French post-war moods, was characteristic of only a small minority of intellectuals, most of them in Paris. But in France, intellectuals have always played a more important role in the formation of public opinion than they do in most other countries. It represented,

[1] *Action*, 27.12.44.
[2] *L'Etre et le Néant.* (Gallimard, 1943), p. 713.

therefore, the conscious and articulate expression of a real pessimism; the measure of the importance of particular forms of pessimism like existentialism and neutralism was not the noise that they made, but the surrounding silence.

The main need of post-war France has been positive ideals to set against similar expressions of negativism. For generations, France has renewed her vitality through the passionate attachment of her citizens to ideas. The second half of the eighteenth century was a time of international and social idealism; the nineteenth century saw the battle for Republicanism and for the separation of Church and State; the first half of the twentieth century saw the fight for economic democracy, the growth of social equality and of educational opportunity, the passionate attachment to democracy of a society of free men who understand the meaning of liberty.

The way ahead? Is 'Europeanism' to be the positive ideal of the 'fifties and 'sixties? That is still far from sure. It arouses fears as well as hopes among politicians, while the general public seems either frankly indifferent, or ill-informed regarding the practical implications of European integration. The dominant mood seems still to be one of political apathy, or disillusionment, attributable to at least three things.

First, the discouragement caused by the complexity of post-war problems, and political divisions and the *immobilisme* of governments, has led some to regard politicians and parties as alike discredited. Gaullism and Poujadism, and sometimes communism, are to some extent forms of escapism—the search for a ready-made solution, whether it be faith in a great man, or in Moscow, or merely retreat into a world of sectional interests or empty slogans.

Second, the mind of post-war France has been further divided, owing to the strength of the impact of the communist philosophy on a number of resisters, particularly intellectuals, who could otherwise have provided the needed positive intellectual leadership. In a sense, this is a sign of vitality, since it represents a reaction against negativism and futility. During the war, many intellectuals had worked in or with communist resistance formations. Their loyalty to communism was all the harder to break in the post-war years owing to the apparent contrast between communist dynamism and unity and the weakness and divisions in the democratic ranks. Communist doctrine helped to fill the intellectual vacuum left by the failure of traditional rationalism and the apparent failure of the classic methods of parliamentary democracy.

Thirdly, the abortive social and economic revolution of the first post-war years and the initial failure of French European policy both helped to create bitterness in precisely those sections of the community that had suffered least from post-war convalescence, that had, on the contrary, been moved by generous impulses and enthusiasms and by a confident hope in the future of France. The bitterness was the more pronounced, perhaps, because these idealists had originally set their sights so high. But its most immediate consequence was that energies which had been, so to speak, side-tracked into over-optimistic and sometimes unrealistic quests, reacted to disappointment by a compensatory over-pessimism. For them, post-war disillusionment meant primarily the sense of being in an intellectual vacuum. Nothing is more painful to a Frenchman. English nature abhors a political vacuum; French nature abhors an intellectual vacuum. The sense of not knowing where one stands, or hopes to go, is as painful as is, to an Englishman, the discovery that no machinery exists to right a recognized wrong.

If to all the other problems there had not been added the essentially insoluble problem posed by the Algerian rebellion, it is possible that, by 1958, the post-war disillusionment might have been very largely overcome. There was in 1953 and 1954 a new note of firmness and directness about some economic thinking; and, in spite of the abortive dissolution of 1955, there was in 1956 and 1957 a much more general recognition of certain constitutional, or parliamentary shortcomings, even if there was not yet agreement on how they could be overcome. But it has been France's tragedy since the war to have encountered, one after the other, problems that have for a time dominated the political stage, yet seemed incapable of solution. Most of them have finally been solved, though not always as France would have wished. The Algerian problem is so grave that some Frenchmen have maintained that failure to solve it could bring a breakdown of the régime. Once again, therefore, in 1958, France is faced with the obligation to make a difficult and painful choice.

APPENDIX I

CHANGES OF GOVERNMENT SINCE THE WAR

(a) DURING THE PERIOD OF PROVISIONAL GOVERNMENT.

Formation of Government	Head of Government	Date of Defeat or Resignation
9 September, 1944 N.B. Algiers Administration reconstituted on return to Paris. Further Government changes: November 1944 May 1945 (after Municipal elections)	General de Gaulle	
21 November, 1945 First Constituent Assembly.	General de Gaulle	20 January 1946 (Resigned)
26 January 1946	Félix Gouin (Soc)	11 June 1946 Referendum 5 May 1946. Elections 2 June 1946
23 June 1946 Second Constituent Assembly.	Georges Bidault (MRP)	28 November 1946 Referendum 13 October Elections 10 November
16 December 1946 Interim Government of Socialists. N.B. Assembly rejected Maurice Thorez (Com) and Georges Bidault (MRP)	Léon Blum (Soc)	16 January 1947 (Resigned on entry into force of 1946 Constitution.)

(b) DURING THE FOURTH REPUBLIC

Date of Investiture of the Prime Minister	Candidates who failed to obtain investiture	Date of defeat or resignation
21 January 1947 Paul Ramadier (Soc) N.B. Government reconstituted without Communists on 9 May 1947; also reconstituted on 22 October after the Municipal elections	21 November 1947 Léon Blum (Soc)	19 November 1947 (Resigned)

225

Date of Investiture of the Prime Minister	Candidates who failed to obtain investiture	Date of defeat or resignation
22 November 1947 Robert Schuman (MRP)		19 July 1948 (Resigned)
24 July 1948 André Marie (Rad)		28 August 1948 (Resigned)
31 August 1948 Robert Schuman (MRP)		7 September 1948 Defeated (but not by constitutional majority) on first meeting with Assembly.
9 September 1948 Henri Queuille (Rad)		5 October 1949 (Resigned)
13 October 1949 Jules Moch (Soc) Failed to constitute a Government. 20 October 1949 René Mayer (Rad) Failed to constitute a Government. 28 October 1949 Georges Bidault (MRP) N.B. Reconstituted Government without Socialists in February 1950		24 June 1950 (Defeated by constitutional majority)
30 June 1950 Henri Queuille (Rad)		4 July 1950 (Defeated on first meeting with Assembly)
11 July 1950 René Pleven (UDSR)		28 February 1951 (Resigned)
	6 March 1951 Guy Mollet (Soc)	
10 March 1951 Henri Queuille (Rad)		10 July 1951 (Resigned after elections)
	25 July 1951 René Mayer (Rad) 2 August 1951 Maurice Petsche (Ind.)	

Date of Investiture of the Prime Minister	Candidates who failed to obtain investiture	Date of defeat or resignation
8 August 1951 René Pleven (UDSR)		*7 January 1952.* (Defeated by constitutional majority)
17 January 1952 Edgar Faure (Rad) *6 March 1952* Antoine Pinay (Rep. Ind.)		*29 February 1952* (Defeated) *23 December 1953.* (Resigned)
7 January 1953 René Mayer (Rad)		*21 May 1953* (Defeated by constitutional majority)
	28 May 1953. Paul Reynaud (Rep. Ind.) *5 June 1953* Pierre Mendès- France (Rad) *11 June 1953* Georges Bidault (MRP) *18 June 1953* André Marie (Rad)	
26 June 1953 Joseph Laniel (Rep. Ind.) *2 January 1954* (Offered resignation after election of new President, remained in office after vote of confidence on 6 January). *17 June 1954* Pierre Mendès-France (Rad)		*12 June 1954* (Defeated)
		5 February 1955 (Defeated by constitutional majority, but after. expiry of 18 months)
23 February 1955 Edgar Faure (Rad)	*19 February 1955* Christian Pineau (Soc)	*29 November 1955* (Dissolved, after defeat by constitutional majority, resigned after elections)
1 February 1956 Guy Mollet (Soc)		*21 May 1957* (Defeated, but not by constitutional majority)

Date of Investiture of the Prime Minister	Candidates who failed to obtain investiture	Date of defeat or resignation
12 June 1957 Maurice Bourgès-Maunoury (Rad)		
		30 September 1957 (Defeated, but not by constitutional majority)
	18 October 1957 Antoine Pinay (Rep. Ind.) *29 October 1957* Guy Mollet (Soc)	
15 November 1957 Félix Gaillard (Rad)		
		16 April 1958 (Defeated, but not on vote of confidence)
14 May 1958 Pierre Pflimlin (MRP)		*18 May 1958* (Resigned)

LIST OF ABBREVIATIONS

A. *Parties and Groups in the Assembly.*

ADS	Groupe de l'Action Démocratique et Sociale.
ARS	Groupe Indépendant d'Action Républicaine et Sociale.
CDS	Groupe du Centre Démocratique Social.
CRIAPS	Groupe du Centre Républicain Indépendant d'Action Paysanne et Sociale.
GI	Groupe de la Gauche Indépendante.
GIP	Groupe Indépendant Paysan.
GP	Groupe Paysan.
GPd'ASR	Groupe Paysan d'Action Sociale et Rurale.
IOM	Groupe des Indépendants d'Outre-Mer.
MRP	Mouvement Républicain Populaire.
MSA	Mouvement Socialiste Africain.
NI	Non-Inscrits.
PC	Parti Communiste.
PRL	Parti Républicain de la Liberté.
PUS	Groupe Paysan et d'Union Sociale.
RAD	Parti Républicain-Radical et Radical-Socialiste.
Rad. diss	Radicaux dissidents.
RDA	Groupe du Rassemblement Démocratique Africain.
RGR	Rassemblement des Gauches Républicaines.
Rep. Ind.	Groupe des Républicains Indépendants.
Rep. Pop. Ind.	Groupe des Républicains Populaires Indépendants.
RPF	Rassemblement du Peuple Français.
Rep. Soc.	Républicains Sociaux.
SFIO	Section Française de l'Internationale Ouvrière (socialist party).
TLDA	Triomphe des Libertés Démocratiques en Algérie.
UDI	Groupe de l'Union Démocratique des Indépendants.
UDSR	Union Démocratique et Socialiste de la Résistance.
UFF (pouj)	Union et Fraternité Française (Poujadist).
URAS	Groupe d'Union Républicaine et d'Action Sociale.
URP	Groupe des Républicains Progressistes. / Union des Républicains Progressistes.

N.B.—The word "groupe" indicates a predominantly, or exclusively parliamentary formation. Others are either national parties with extra-parliamentary organizations, or electoral combinations.

B. *Trade Union Movements.*

CCN	Comité Confédéral National.
CFTC	Confédération Française des Travailleurs Chrétiens.
CGA	Confédération Générale de l'Agriculture.
CGC	Confédération Générale des Cadres.
CGT	Confédération Générale du Travail.
CGT-FO	Confédération Générale du Travail—Force Ouvrière.
CNPF	Conseil National du Patronat Français.
CNT	Confédération Nationale du Travail.
CTI	Confédération des Travailleurs Indépendants.

Parties in the Assembly 1951–1957

	Jan. 1951	Jan. 1952	Jan. 1954	Jan. 1956	Oct. 1957
PC	167	97	96	144	143
URP (GRP)	7(4)	4	4	5(1)	5(1)
RDA	6	—	—	—	—
TLDA	3	—	—	—	—
SFIO	99	104(2)	104(1)	94(1)	96(1)
MSA	—	—	—	—	3(1)
Rad.	42(3)	68(8)	69(7)	54(4)	42(1)
UDSR	12(3)	16(7)	16(9)	—	—
UDSR-RDA	—	—	—	18(1)	18(3)
RGR	—	—	—	10(4)	9(4)
Rad. diss.	—	—	—	—	14
MRP	145	85(3)	82(5)	70(3)	71(4)
IOM	11(1)	12	15	10	7
GI	3	—	—	—	—
Rep. Ind.	24(1)	45(9)	48(6)	80(3)	86(6)
PUS	—	19(4)	—	—	—
CRIAPS	19(1)	19(3)	—	—	—
GIP	—	—	24(4)	—	—
GP	—	—	14	12	10(2)
GPd'ASR	—	—	—	—	6
UDI	7	—	—	—	—
CDS	—	—	5	—	—
PRL	27(2)	—	—	—	—
ADS(RPF)	16(1)	—	—	—	—
Rep. Pop. Ind. (app)	6	—	—	—	—
RPF	—	114(3)	—	—	—
ARS	—	32(2)	—	—	—
URAS	—	—	77	—	—
Rep. Soc.	—	—	—	20(1)	19(2)
UFF (Pouj.)	—	—	—	51(1)	30
NI	9	5	6	6	10
Vacant	2	—	1	3	2
Others	—	—	—	30 (not elected)	30 (not elected)
Total	622	627	627	626	626

N.B.—Group memberships are given as published at the beginning of each session. Horizontal lines show the division into the six major groupings. Relations between groups within such groupings varies. Thus the *Indépendants d'Outre-Mer* has been at times independent, at others, *apparenté* to the MRP. Figures in brackets represent independent deputies who are *apparentés* to the group.

POSTSCRIPT

The crisis of the régime. The long-predicted crisis of the régime, which the deadlocks described in the preceding chapters seemed to render sooner or later inevitable, became a fact in the spring of 1958. In the early hours of 16 April the third government since the general election of January 1956 fell, having wrestled unsuccessfully, like its predecessors, with the financial and international repercussions of France's difficulties in North Africa and, in particular, with the insoluble problem presented by the Algerian rebellion. After a month (the third month of governmental interregnum within a year) the prospect of a government headed by M. Pflimlin (MRP) was the signal for hostile demonstrations by the European population of Algiers (and for demonstrations on a smaller scale in Paris), the right-wing settlers regarding M. Pflimlin's party as being prepared to 'abandon' Algeria, because many of its members held liberal views, including approval of an eventual federal relationship between France and Algeria. The leaders of the demonstrators set up a Committee of Public Safety, which included both Europeans and Moslems, and also some French army officers—in particular, General Massu, commander of the paratroop division and of the Algiers region. After their failure to prevent the investiture of M. Pflimlin, in the early hours of 14 May, they demanded the constitution of a Government of Public Safety under the direction of General de Gaulle, if he were willing to accept office. The movement had become an insurrection.

For some days it was not clear whether General Massu

and his superior officer, General Salan, Commander-in-Chief in Algeria, were leading the rebellion, or, as later became the official thesis, had joined the movement in order to control it, or to prevent civil war. During the following fortnight, Committees of Public Safety were set up throughout Algeria; on 24 May the insurrection spread to Corsica; and Radio Algiers threatened risings and the establishment of similar committees in France.

M. Pflimlin's Government took a number of emergency measures. Some small extreme right-wing organizations were dissolved; the Assembly granted the Government emergency powers for three months; the reserve *gendarmerie* was mobilized and, after the Corsican insurrection, police reinforcements were drafted to towns in the South of France. The proposals for constitutional reform, then under consideration (see p. 32), were modified so as to extend the Government's power of delegated legislation and to limit parliamentary sessions to five months in the year.

In spite of these and other efforts to strengthen the hands of the Government, a chain of political reactions helped to weaken it. First, support for the insurrection from a handful of parliamentary leaders in the Assembly, and, more important, the threat by three of the four right-wing ministers to resign unless General de Gaulle were approached, helped to cancel out the impression of governmental and parliamentary solidarity that the Government had hoped to create as a result of the Socialist party's decision to join the Government.[1] The communiqué issued by General de Gaulle, on 27 May, after his meeting with M. Pflimlin, seemed to indicate, rather, that the Government was preparing to abdicate.

[1] The party had decided on 2 May not to participate in any Government during the lifetime of the Parliament.

For General de Gaulle stated that he had 'set in motion the regular procedure necessary for the establishment of a Republican Government capable of ensuring the unity and independence of the country'. At this time M. Pflimlin's Government was still in office.

On the other hand, the cohesion of the insurrectionaries was increased by this communiqué, since it appeared to indicate that their victory was in sight; and they had been considerably helped, too, by General de Gaulle's two previous statements, the first, on 15 May, expressing his willingness 'to assume the powers of the Republic'; the second, on 19 May, amplifying this by information regarding the conditions in which he was prepared to do so, and giving explicit approval to the behaviour of the army in Algeria.

In fact, General de Gaulle's statements did three things. They strengthened the insurrection, by canalizing what were, in reality, a number of conflicting tendencies, into a movement whose main immediate objective was his return to power; they helped to undermine the resistance of Republican opinion in France to this eventuality, because he gave categoric reassurances that he would assume only those powers delegated to him by the Republic, and that he would respect Republican legality; and they increased the fears of many Frenchmen, by no means all on the Right, that the only alternative to General de Gaulle might be a Popular Front. For the immediate reaction of the Communist party and the Communist-dominated trade union leaders was to call for strikes and the establishment of workers' 'anti-Fascist' committees. After years of attempts to sabotage parliamentary government and to weaken the Republic they were now ready to rush vocally to its defence.

Another factor that helped to weaken the Government

was the sudden, belated, and hysterical conversion of the Algerian European population, and also apparently of some Moslems, to a policy of 'integration', that is, of complete equality, political, economic and social, between the two races. After three weeks of mass meetings in the Algiers Forum, characterized by speech-making, frenzied flag-waving, slogan-shouting, and emotional demonstrations of Franco-Moslem fraternization, many Frenchmen, who had at first been sceptical—or had suspected the whole movement of having been 'rigged' by the European extremists in Algeria for their own ends— were convinced that some miraculous sea-change really had occurred. This was bound, obviously, to strengthen the hands of the Right, which included the more fanatical believers in *l'Algérie française*, and whose support for M. Pflimlin was already less than lukewarm. For the first time the idea of a French Algeria seemed to many Frenchmen a practical possibility instead of an outdated fiction.

The Government was weakened, too, by fears of the unreliability of the army and of the security police, or, at least, by its reluctance, either through fear or through the desire to avoid any danger of clashes between Frenchmen, to put this reliability to the test. Whether threats from Algiers of possible risings in France, on the model of that in Corsica, were genuine, or were partly bluff, French Deputies' fears of them were certainly real enough. And so, in the early hours of 28 May, though he had just been given an overwhelming vote of confidence, which his predecessors in office would have regarded as a triumph, M. Pflimlin resigned. The President of the Republic's message to the two Assemblies on the following day no doubt helped to overcome the last resistance, which came from the Socialists. He spoke of France as being "on the verge of civil war" and added that he would feel compelled to resign if the Assembly did not invest General de Gaulle, whom he had asked to try to form a government. On 1 June, the Assembly voted General de Gaulle into office by 329 votes to 224, an opposition which included 147 Communists and their associates and 49 Socialists. Forty-two Socialists voted for him.

There followed a series of rapid and far-reaching decisions of which the most important were the delegation by the Assembly to the Government of special powers to legislate for six months, while Parliament went into recess until the normal opening of the session in October;[1] the revision of article 90 of the constitution, empowering the Government to submit a revised constitution to a referendum (after consulting a committee, two-thirds of whose members would be Deputies and Senators); the announcement, after a three-day tour of Algeria by General de Gaulle, that local elections would be held there in a month and that the constitutional referendum would take place in October, and the completion of a governmental team which, to the surprise of many in France, and to the dismay of the Algiers insurrectionaries, included representatives of all political parties except the Communists and the Poujadists (including three ex-Prime Ministers, MM. Pinay, Pflimlin, and Mollet), a number of highly respected officials, not openly associated with any party, but no personality in

[1] The powers were not unlimited. They specifically excluded measures affecting fundamental political liberties, criminal procedure and penalties, property and social rights, the electoral law and matters that Republican constitutional tradition considered as belonging exclusively to the field of legislation. The President of the Assembly also reminded Deputies that the Assembly remained technically in session until the pronouncement of the closure under article 9.

any way associated with the insurrection. This appeared to be a Republican government, whose task was to be the liquidation of the Fourth Republic.

After the Fourth Republic—what? Whether the Fourth Republic was to be replaced by a Fifth, or by some authoritarian régime, was a question to which nobody, in June 1958, knew the answer. What people were mainly conscious of was their lack of information regarding a number of factors in the extremely confusing situation in which General de Gaulle had returned to power. There were, in particular, three major enigmas. The first was Algeria. Was the new demand for 'integration' genuine? It appeared to be in flat contradiction with previous attitudes of the right-wing settlers now demanding it, for they had always bitterly opposed the most moderate reforms designed to improve the status of Moslems. And even if it were genuine, how could France possibly afford the cost—estimated by one neutral source to amount to £800,000,000 a year (leaving out of account the increasing birthrate in Algeria), that is, more than the cost of the military campaign that was crippling French finances? How far could the army succeed in restoring the authority of the French State over the European insurrectionaries? And even if it did, was the political climate in Algeria such as to persuade wavering or uncommitted Moslems to have confidence in France (or at least in General de Gaulle), or to persuade the Moslem rebels to accept General de Gaulle's offer of reconciliation, and to transform themselves into a legal opposition party by voting in the elections? And even if either of these changes were conceivable, could Moslems rely on elections free from all pressure and intimidation?

The second enigma was General de Gaulle himself. The former President of the Republic, M. Auriol, said that he had greatly changed, but in what respects? Did his apparent readiness to co-operate with politicians of 'the system', that he had so severely criticized, represent a change, or merely a stepping-off ground? Once securely in the saddle, would he be led, voluntarily or involuntarily, to adopt more authoritarian methods? If he did not succeed in his aim of reducing the illegal Committees of Public Safety to the status of propaganda adjuncts of the regularly constituted authorities, might he not end by becoming the prisoner of the army, or of an insurrectionary movement, or of both, instead of a national leader? Was his Government likely to draw up a constitution, acceptable at the same time to him and to Republican opinion? He had assured Deputies that he no longer believed in the Presidential system (which he had approved of in his Bayeux speech of 16 June 1946); but nothing had been said to the Assembly about his attitude regarding either corporatist ideas, such as '*l'association capital-travail*' or functional representation in the Second Chamber. He had undertaken, in the law revising article 90, to recognize the principle of universal suffrage, the responsibility of the Government to Parliament, the independence of the judiciary, and the separation of legislative and executive power. Were these guarantees sufficient? The most urgent question of all was that of the real meaning of his oracular and ambiguous statements in Algeria. Was he in favour of integration, of a French Algeria, of a North African federation, of a negotiated, or an imposed settlement? The absence of clear guidance on these points, and the presence of a great deal of wishful thinking, led to contradictory deductions, the result of which was bound to be the disillusionment of considerable sections of opinion when the mystery was finally cleared up.

There was also the enigma of French public opinion. The average French citizen, who during these three May weeks that shook the Western world had preserved an unshaken calm and had appeared not to care how, or by whom, he was governed, would have, if General de Gaulle kept his promise, the last word in deciding what was to be France's future constitution. His apparent indifference up to then was a consequence of the Fourth Republic's successes as well as of its failings. For during the years from 1953 onwards, when political problems were being increasingly evaded, economic problems were being successfully tackled. Production was increasing, standards of living of the workers were improving, and there was greater industrial peace. Citizens might be passive, if it were merely a matter of discredited politicians losing their jobs. But would they remain so if it became a matter of French citizens losing their Republican liberties? There was little evidence, in June 1958, of enthusiasm for authoritarianism, but some 200,000 Parisians did demonstrate, on 28 May, in favour of Republicanism.

The one undisputed fact, in a situation full of doubts, speculations, unanswered questions, and anxious heart-searchings, was that, as he himself said, at Constantine on 5 June, General de Gaulle bore 'heavy responsibilities to the country, to history, and to God'. Not the least among them was the responsibility of enlightening his country-men regarding his intentions. As and when it became possible for him to do so, it would be possible for them to decide whether to fight with him or against him as circumstances demanded, for the final supremacy of that one of *les deux Frances*, whose hopes and failures had been symbolized by the creation, and the fall, of four Republics.

A SHORT BIBLIOGRAPHY

1. The background.

Brogan, D. W. *The Development of Modern France* (*1870–1939*). Hamish Hamilton, 1940.
The French Nation 1814–1940. Hamish Hamilton, 1957.
Bury, J. P. T. *France 1814–1940.* Methuen, 1949.
Maillaud, Pierre. *France.* Oxford University Press, 1942.
Pickles, Dorothy. *France between the Republics.* Contact Publications, 1946.
Thomson, David. *Democracy in France.* Oxford University Press, 1950.
Goguel, François. *La Politique des Partis sous la IIIe République.* Editions du Seuil, 1946.
Siegfried, André. *Tableau des Partis en France.* Grasset, 1930.
Thibaudet, Albert. *Les Idées politiques de la France.* Stock, 1932.

2. Institutions and Political Parties in the Fourth Republic.

Campbell, Peter. *French electoral systems and elections, 1789–1957.* Faber and Faber, 1958.
Chapman, B. *Introduction to French Local Government.* Allen and Unwin, 1953.
The Prefects and Provincial France. Allen and Unwin, 1955.
Goguel, François. *France under the Fourth Republic.* Cornell University Press, 1952.
Einaudi, Domenach and Garosci. *Communism in Western Europe.* University of Notre Dame Press, 1951.
Einaudi and Goguel. *Christian Democracy in Italy and France.* University of Notre Dame Press, 1952.
Lidderdale, D. W. S. *The Parliament of France.* The Hansard Society, 1951.
Pickles, Dorothy. *French Politics, The First Years of the Fourth Republic.* Royal Institute of International Affairs, 1953.

Williams, Philip. *Politics in post-war France.* Longmans, 1954.

Brayance, Alain. *Anatomie du Parti communiste français.* Denoël, 1952.

Deschamps, Hubert. *Méthodes et doctrines coloniales de la France.* Paris, Colin, 1953.

Duverger, Maurice. *Droit Public.* Paris, Presses Universitaires de France, 1957.

Fauvet, Jacques. *Les Forces Politiques en France.* Le Monde, 1951.

Goguel, François. *Le Régime politique français.* Paris, Editions du Seuil, 1955.

Prélot, Marcel. *Précis de droit constitutionnel.* Paris, Dalloz, 1952.

Rolland, Louis. *Précis de droit administratif.* Paris, Dalloz, 1951.

Siegfried, André. *De la IIIᵉ à la IVᵉ République.* Paris, Grasset, 1956.

3. *Economic and foreign problems.*

France, Overseas Economic Surveys, London. H.M. Stationery Office, 1953.

Labour-Management Cooperation in France. I.L.O., Geneva, 1950.

Robson, W. A. *Nationalized Industries in Britain and France.* American Political Science Review, June 1950.

Chenot, Bernard. *L'Organisation économique de l'Etat.* Paris, Dalloz, 1951.

France économique 1956. Revue d'économie politique, Numéro spécial. Juillet–Octobre 1957.

Jeanneney, J. M. *Forces et Faiblesses de l'économie françaises.* Paris, Armand Colin, 1956.

La Nef. Le franc, mythe et réalité, La Nef-Julliard, 1953. *Le Problème allemand.* La Nef-Julliard, 1952.

INDEX